GW01605731

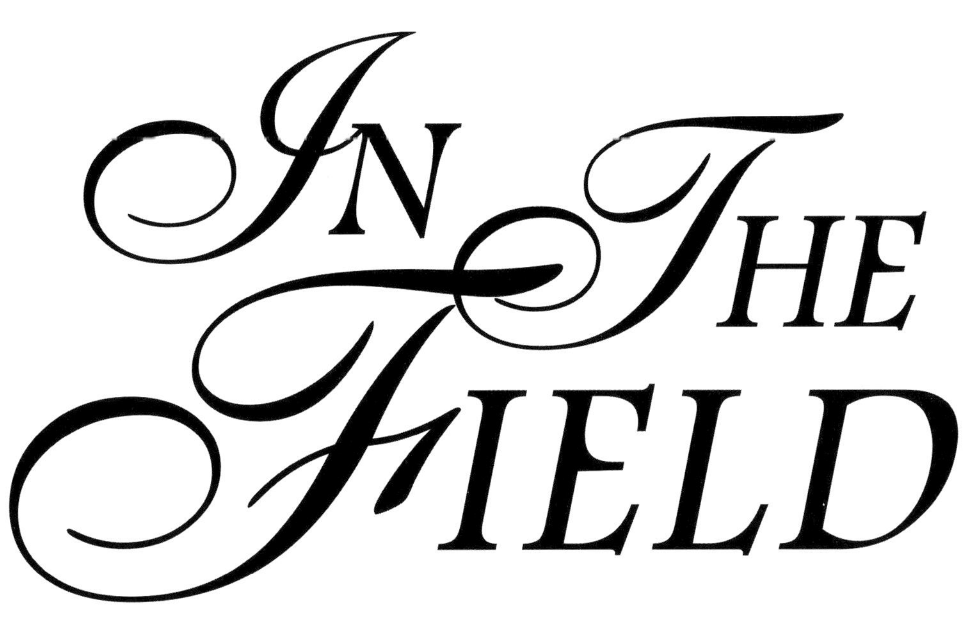
IN THE FIELD

In the Field

Published by Wudcahk Publishing

Wudcahk Publishing

First Printing 2008

All Photography by
Nancy Whitehead

Wudcahk Publishing
PO Box 3023
Hailey, Idaho 83333

Sporting Dog Photography
www.sportingdogphotography.com

Book production by Mark Kashino
kashino.com

ISBN: 978-0-615-24717-5

Library of Congress Control Number: 2008939684

Printed in Canada

Nancy Whitehead is available
for assignment photography.
To see more images of Nancy's
work or to order fine art gallery prints,
please log on to our website at:
www.sportingdogphotography.com

Cover Photograph:
Champion Elhew Explorer,
Owned by John and Mel Pfeifle,
Hampshire Kennels
Bradford, New Hampshire

Back Cover Photograph:
Justright Tabatha JH
Owned by Jack & Joan Crawford,
Spring Island, South Carolina

Dedication

For my grandchildren Colby, Gage, Kelby, Piper, Reide, and Slater
in a tradition of family and dogs that will continue always.

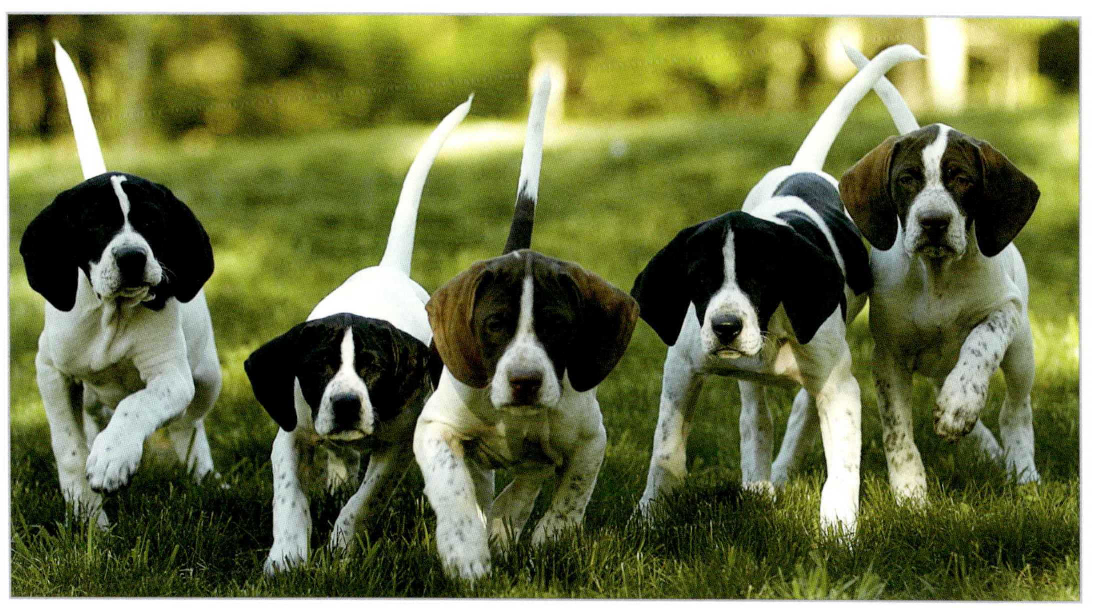

9/2017
To Anthony &
Teresa,
With much love to two
People who love the hunt!
Many thanks for your love &
friendship.
Judy

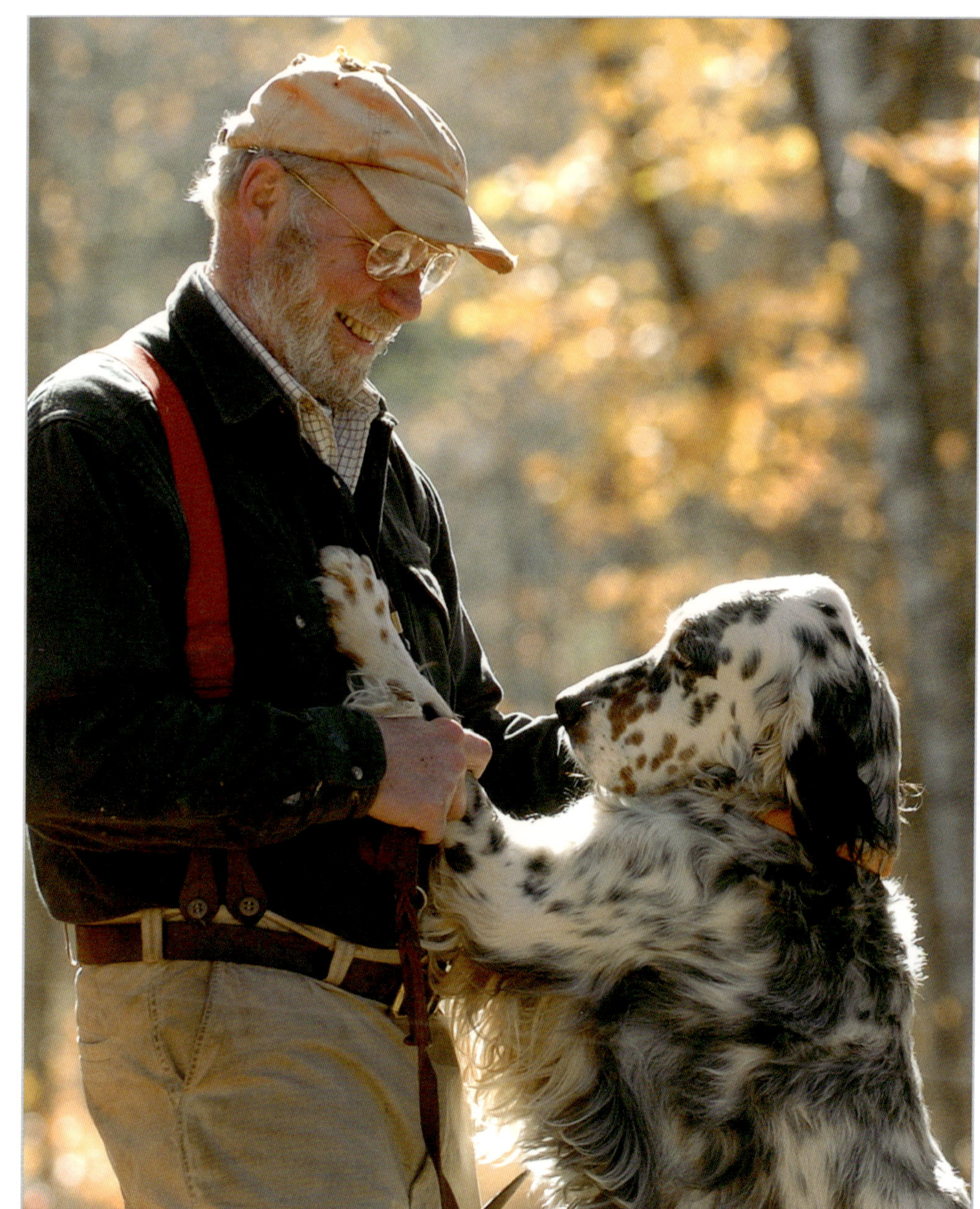

I think we are drawn to dogs because
they are the uninhibited creatures we might be
if we weren't certain we knew better.
~George Bird Evans

Acknowledgements

I would like to thank in alphabetical order Ken Alexander of Decoverly Kennels, Scott Boettger, Walter and Sandi Boomer, Bradley Carleton, Jack and Joan Crawford, Gary Currier, Cheryl and Alan Higham, Dick Hinman, Bud Isaac, Sally Kern, Jim Kennedy, John Lesher, Steve McCoy, Wilson and Lisa McElliney, John Oliver, Gren and Jo Schock, Warren Sims, Valhalla Bijou Kennels, and Iris Winthrop of the Groton Plantation, for the opportunity to be able photograph such magnificent dogs in beautiful places.

Special thanks to those wonderful talented and dedicated dog trainers Shawn Kinkaleer, Harold Ray and Doug Ray, for their time and patience.

To Les Lahring of Valhalla Bijou Kennels, Charlie and Nancy Metz of Shooting Stars Farm and Fred and Bernice Rowan of Cassique Plantation a very special thanks!

John and Mel Pfeifle of Hampshire Kennels for their continued support, the abundance of memories and their beautiful dogs!

To my boys Gunnar and Peter and the cold mornings on the Snake River and all the other wonderful shared times and memorable moments with dogs! To my husband Bill for constant support and companionship and the fun we have had on our photographic journeys!

Finally, to Charles Gaines and Laurie Sammis for keeping me on track as much as they were able! I could not have even contemplated finishing this project without both of you!

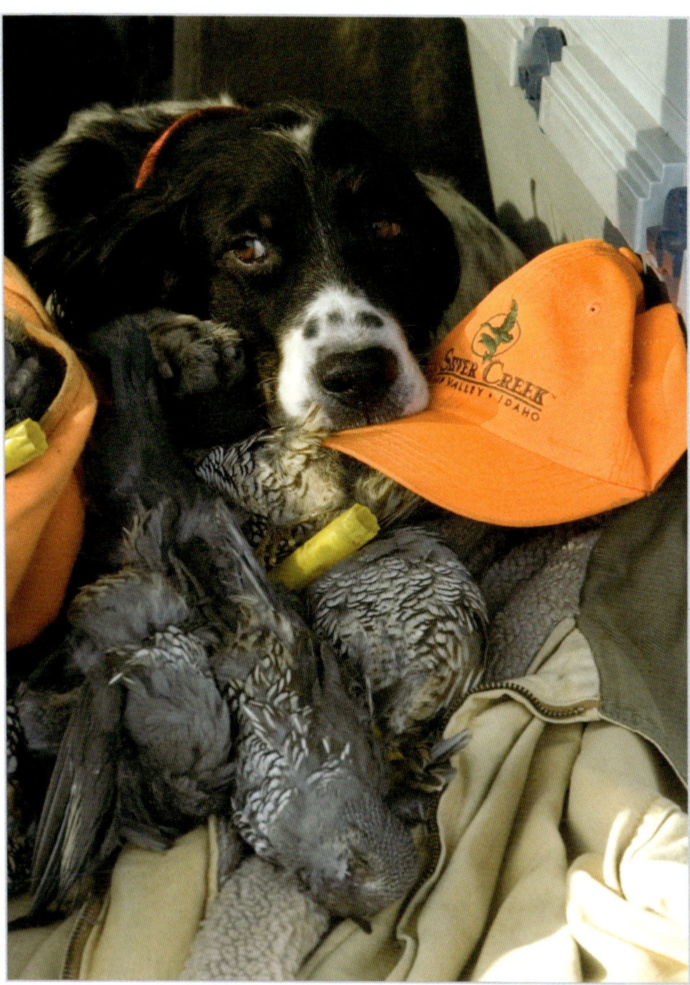

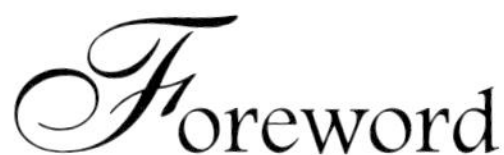

Foreword

Like the best bird dogs, the best photographers wear their hearts on their sleeves. Passion is too pale a word to describe what both bring to their predatory lines of work. Complete immersion is more like it: a good bird dog ***is*** its nose tracking scent; a good photographer, an eye hunting images. Everything else to either is just lying around the kennel.

In 1973 Annie Liebowitz was sent to Johannesburg, South Africa by *Rolling Stone* magazine to photograph the making of the documentary film, "Pumping Iron." Virtually unknown back then, Annie was a tall, shy, endearingly gangly girl who ran pretty much at low idle except when she was photographing the equally unknown star of the film, Arnold Schwarzenegger. Then she would red-line into an unnervingly different creature – intense, imperious, proprietary, and inexhaustible – as she tracked Arnold like a Shorthair on a cornfield pheasant throughout his preparations for that year's Mr. Olympia contest. When her pictures of him came out in *Rolling Stone*, I remember looking at them and thinking: So ***this*** is what photography is – the retrieving of some deeply personal vision of the truth and offering it up as unassailably real and immediate as a warm bird in a Lab's mouth.

In the introduction to a book by Mary Ellen Mark – another brilliant female photographer I have had the pleasure of knowing – the curator Marianne Fulton writes that "Great photographers know what their subjects are," and that they are able to marry that necessary subject matter with a distinctive and appropriate form to create what in writing is called "voice." It is this voice that enables us to feel we are seeing the subject matter of great photographs, no matter how familiar, for the first time.

I would argue that Nancy Whitehead's pictures in this book are just such photographs. What the circus people of India were to Mary Ellen and celebrities to Annie, gun dogs are here to Nancy – the exactly correct subject matter for the exactly correct form – and the unique photographic voice she has created offers up the truth of that subject matter more clearly and immediately, I believe, than it has ever been offered up before.

It is no surprise that bird dogs would become Nancy's subject. She has been in love with them since she was a child following her father's setters through New Hampshire coverts. When I got to know her in that state over two decades ago, she and her friend, the trainer and breeder Mel Pfeifle were covered up in bird dogs, and both have remained that way, even after Nancy and her family moved to Idaho. She and I had lost touch with each other by then, but when she called one day out of the blue to say that she had taken up photography and to ask if I would look at some of her pictures, I pretty much knew before she told me what would be in them.

"Well...yeah. Sure," is what I told her, probably in the same tone of voice I tend to fall into with people who ask me if I'll read the 600-page handwritten memoir they have just finished. Because what I did ***not*** know, had no way of knowing, was how drop-dead ravishing those pictures would be.

I too have been in love with bird dogs since childhood. I have owned and trained (or failed to train) more than a dozen of them, and could probably remember the names of a hundred – English and wirehaired pointers, English, Gordon and Irish setters, German shorthairs, Brittanys,

Goldens, Labs, Springers and English cockers – whom I have had the honor to sit beside in a blind or walk behind in a field or woods over the years. Curled up on a leather couch in my study as I write this are a cocker and a setter. On the walls and desks of the study are no fewer than a dozen photographs of bird dogs, and on its shelves at least twice that many books that deal with them in one way or another. Bird dogs, in short, are a blessed part of my quotidian, and have been for over half a century. And yet in this book they look brand new to me – as exotic and glamorous and fresh to my eye as runway models.

It is, of course, part of the job description of good art to make the familiar new and free of cliché (there is not a single trite photo in these pages, not even of puppies). Another, more difficult, part is to direct our attention to a particular tension of elements, a particular vitality of relating parts that becomes, through repetition, its own language. The language of these luscious, evocative photographs is both rich and spare at the same time, like that of Homer's paintings. It is a painterly rather than pictorial language, full of honeyed prairie light and southeastern fogs, and yet it is never sentimental or overblown, being held to account by strong, elegant compositions: such as the sweet line formed by a woman's arm, a dead quail and a Lab's head and shoulders; such as a rider, a dog on point and a horizon framed by a horse's ears.

The content of the pictures is similarly disciplined and balanced between the rich and the spare – from the effulgence of a flock of mallards erupting off a pond to a single butterfly perched on a clover flower. In addition to the dogs, there are men, women and children in these photos, and boats and horses and guns and duck blinds, prairies and marshes and upland woods and lakes and rivers, yet none of the pictures seem crowded. Instead each resonates with a lean specificity, and many – because of the rigorous control of content – with a whelming sense of place.

Whatever the content of these pictures, the subject of all of them – quite gloriously – is gun dogs (even, somehow, in those pictures in which no dog appears). I can think of no higher compliment for the book's treatment of that subject than to say it is so intimate, so empathetic and expressive of those creatures' particular grace and beauty in the performance of their work that it almost seems to have been photographed by one. When I first looked at Nancy's pictures, I wondered how she could possibly get what's going on between the two pointers wrapped in that beautiful frozen *pas de deux* of point and back, or that look of regal "gotcha" on the face of another pointer standing steady to wing and ***watching*** a woodcock rise to the gun, without at least speaking Dog?

Then two autumns ago Nancy came up to New Brunswick to take pictures on the annual grouse and woodcock trip I have been making to that province for 25 years, and I found out. I am tempted to say it is with "doggedness;" and in fact it was with that, as she followed me and my long-legged young friends tirelessly for days through the alder and poplar thickets. But more importantly, it is with the Annie Liebowitz thing: Nancy gets the magic, and truth, of bird dogs that distinguishes these pages by being completely submerged, lost to the world, in her hunt for it; and by wearing, like the dogs she photographs, her heart on her sleeve as she does it.

Charles Gaines
Monastery, Nova Scotia
June, 2008

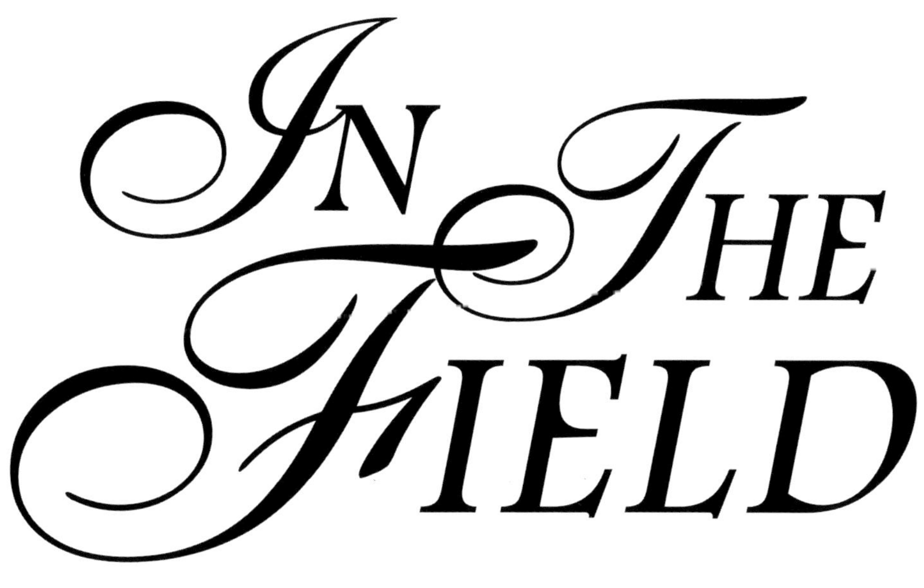

A Photographer's Journey with Sporting Dogs

Nancy Whitehead

Portraits

I would rather see the portrait of a dog that I know,
than all the allegorical paintings they can show me in the world.
~Samuel Johnson

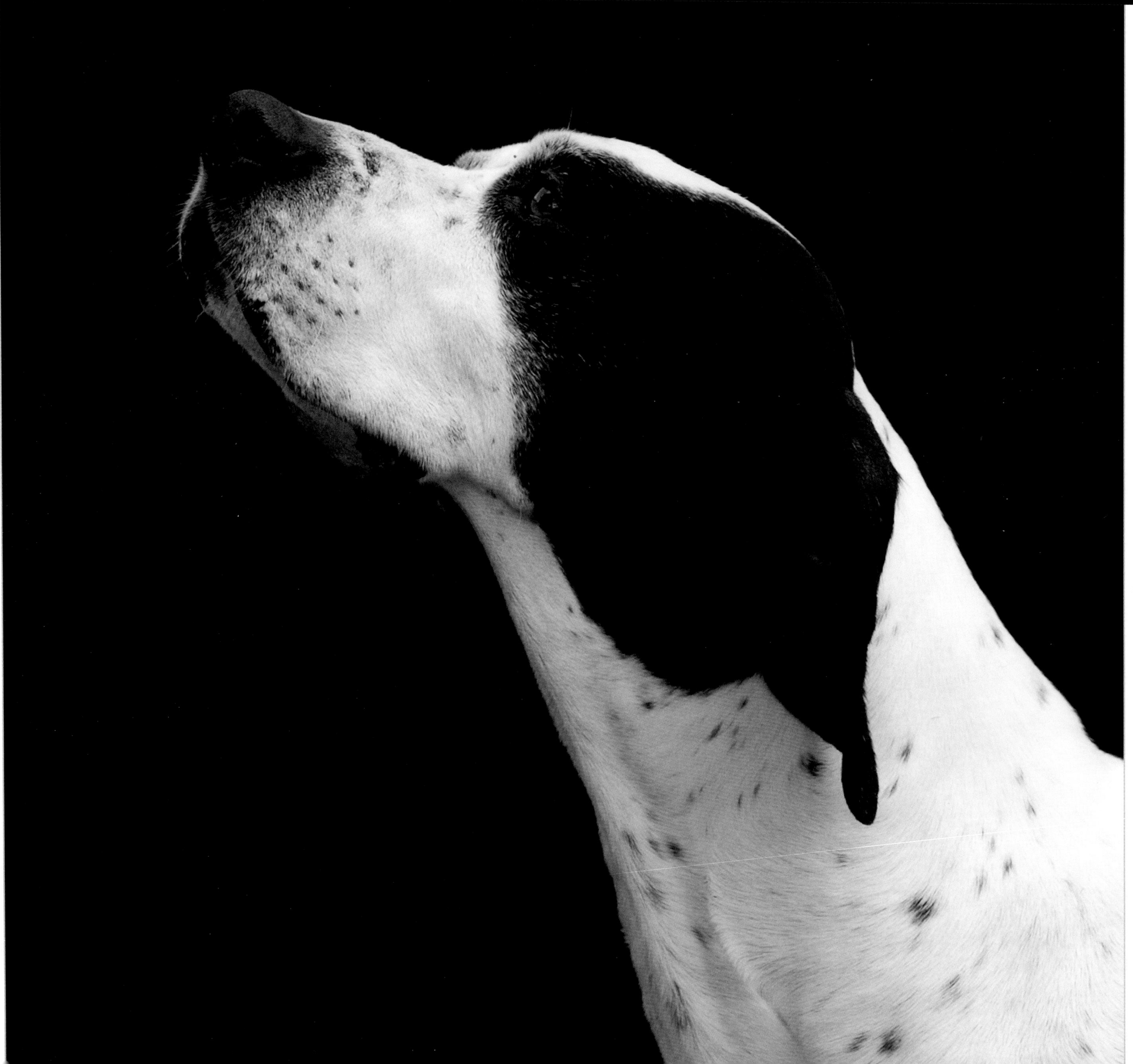

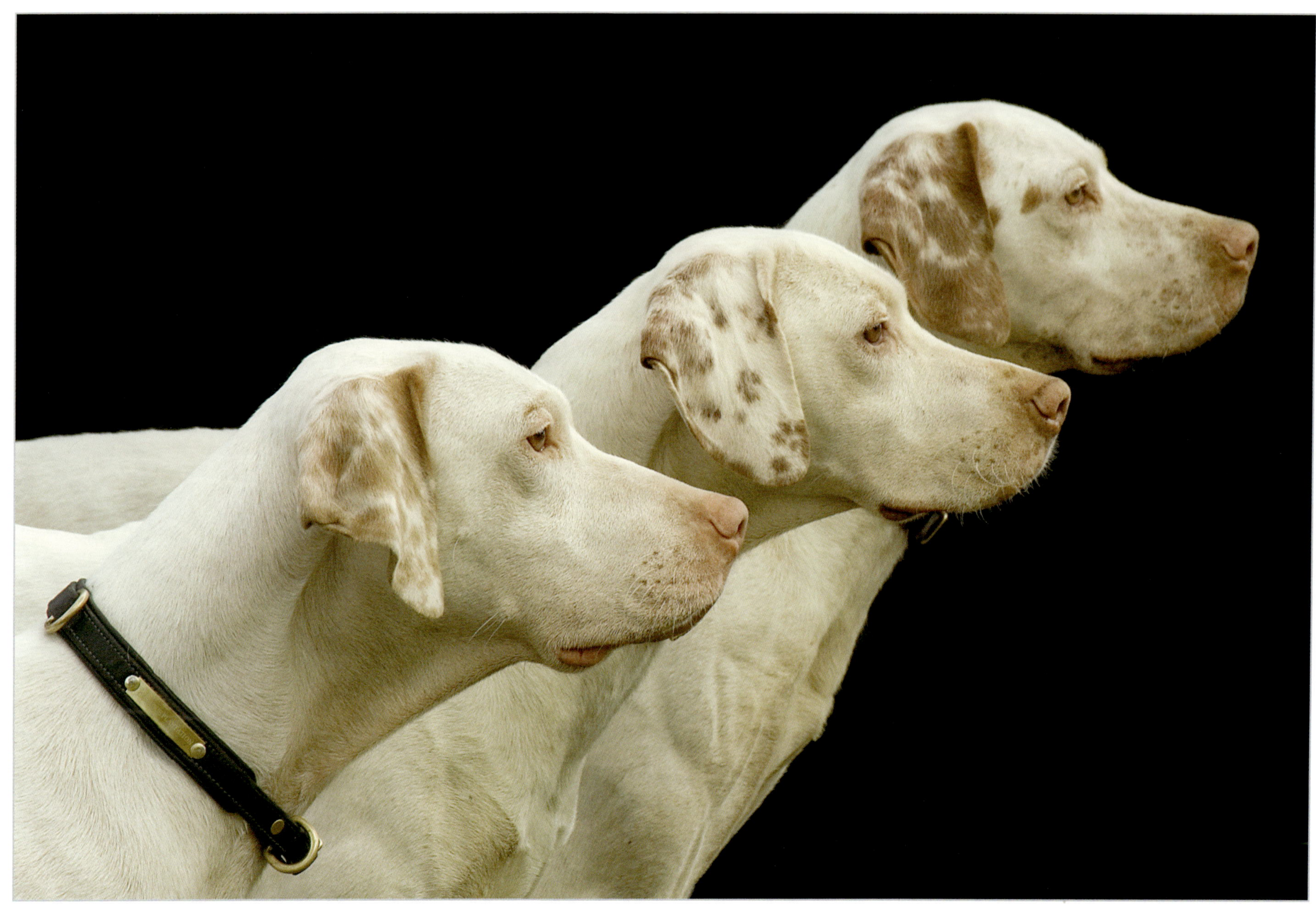

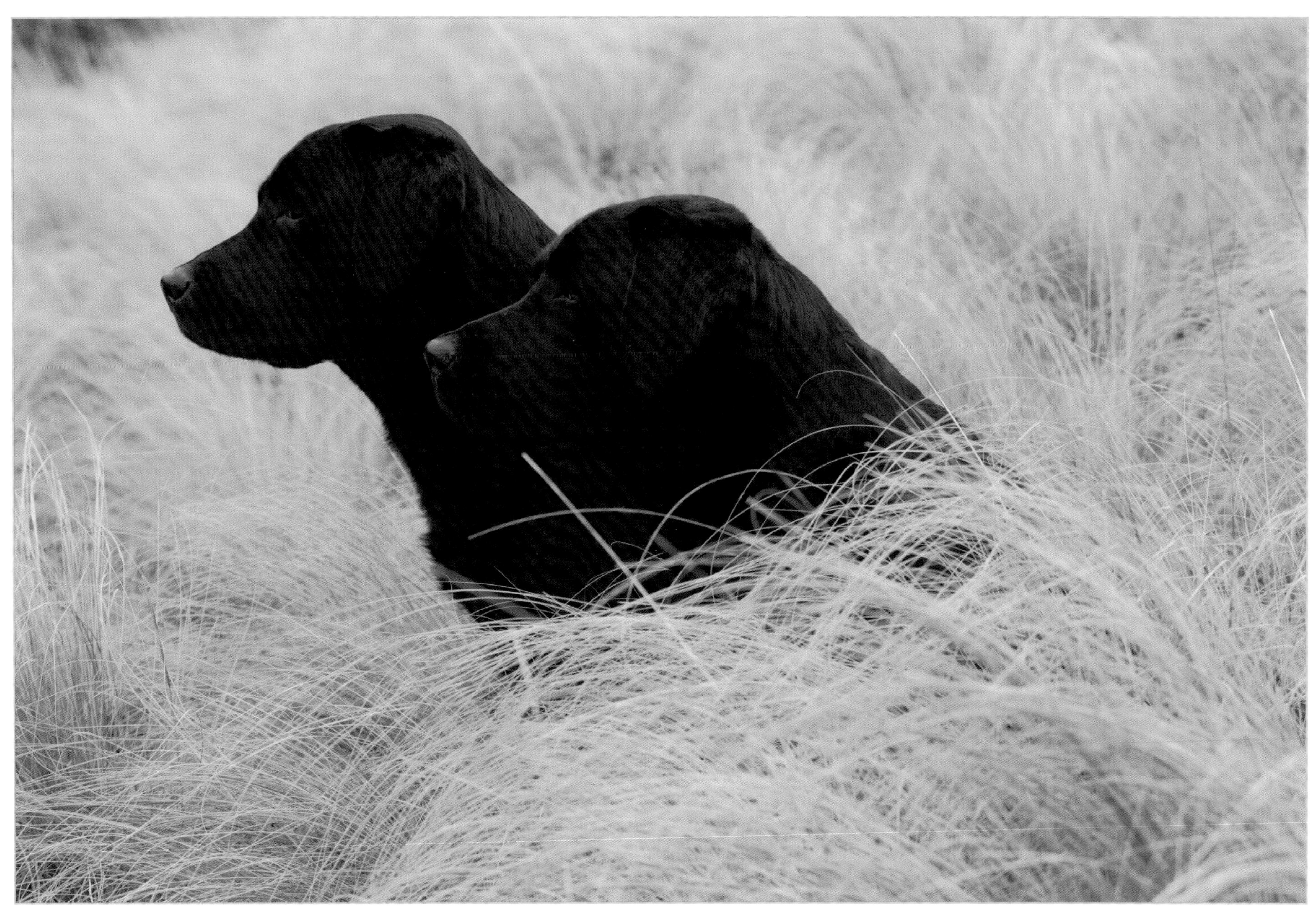

The moment one gives close attention to any thing, even a blade of grass, it becomes a mysterious, awesome indescribably magnificent world in itself. ~Henry Miller

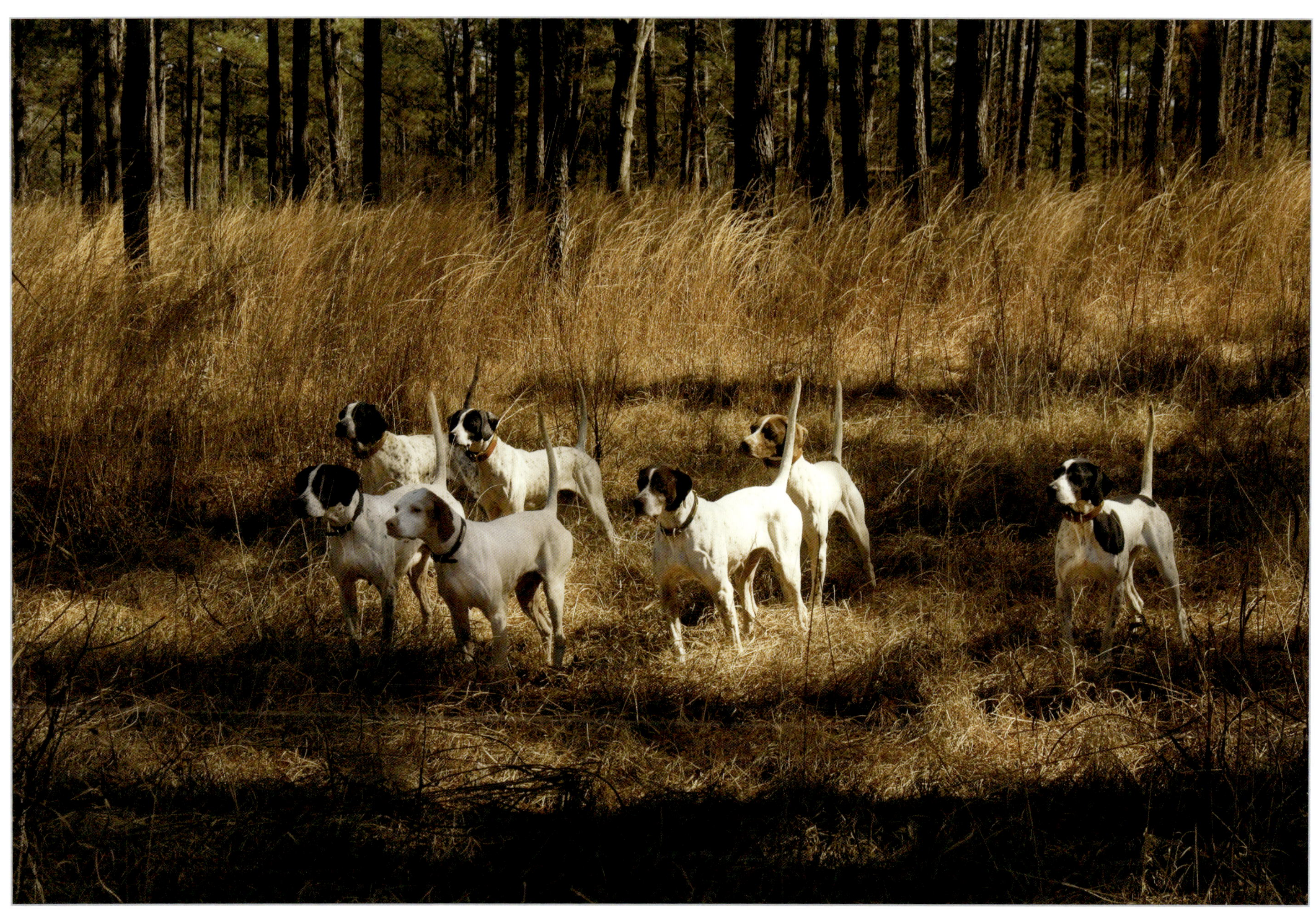

What is required is sight and insight—then you might add one more: excite. ~Robert Frost

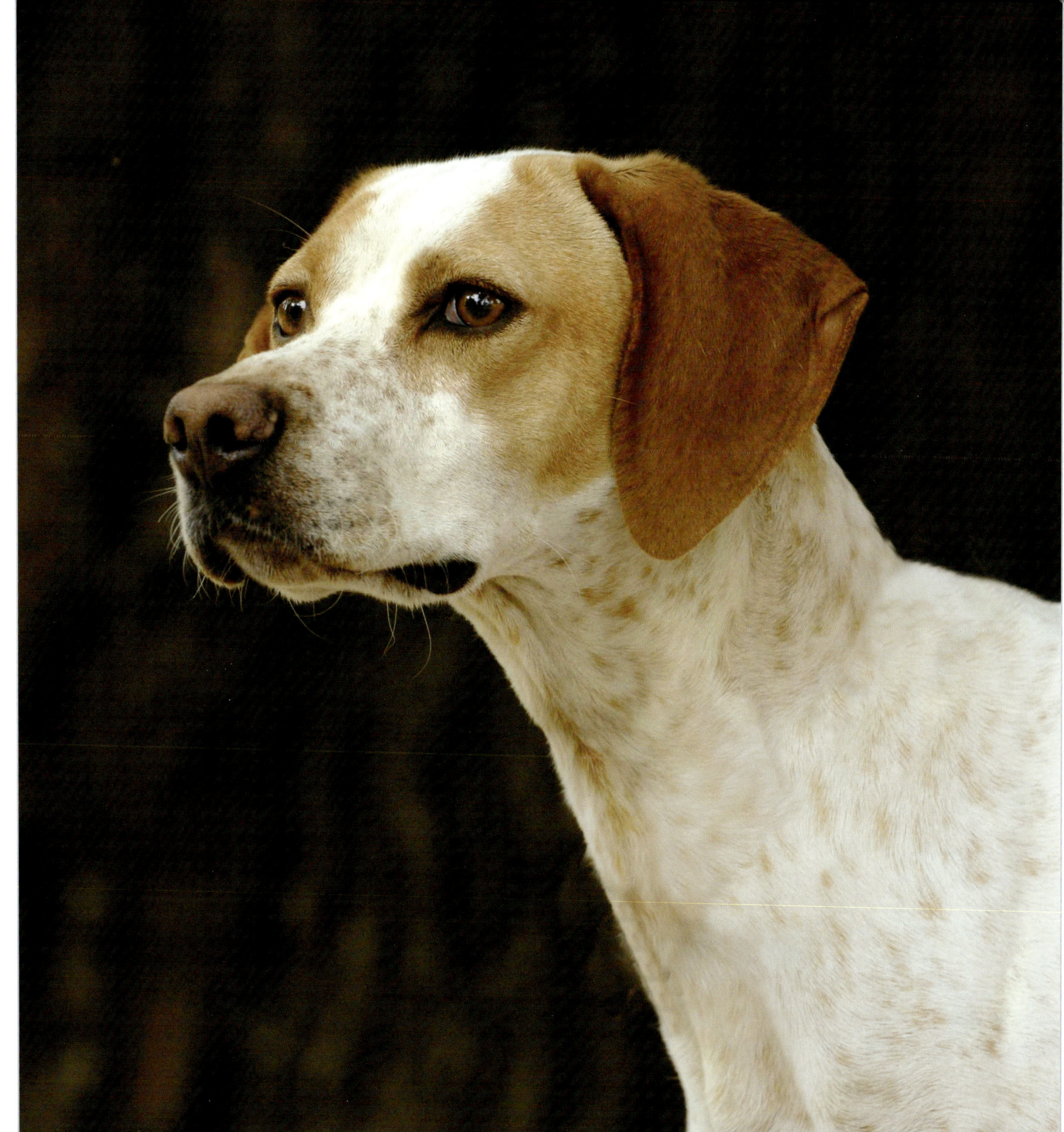

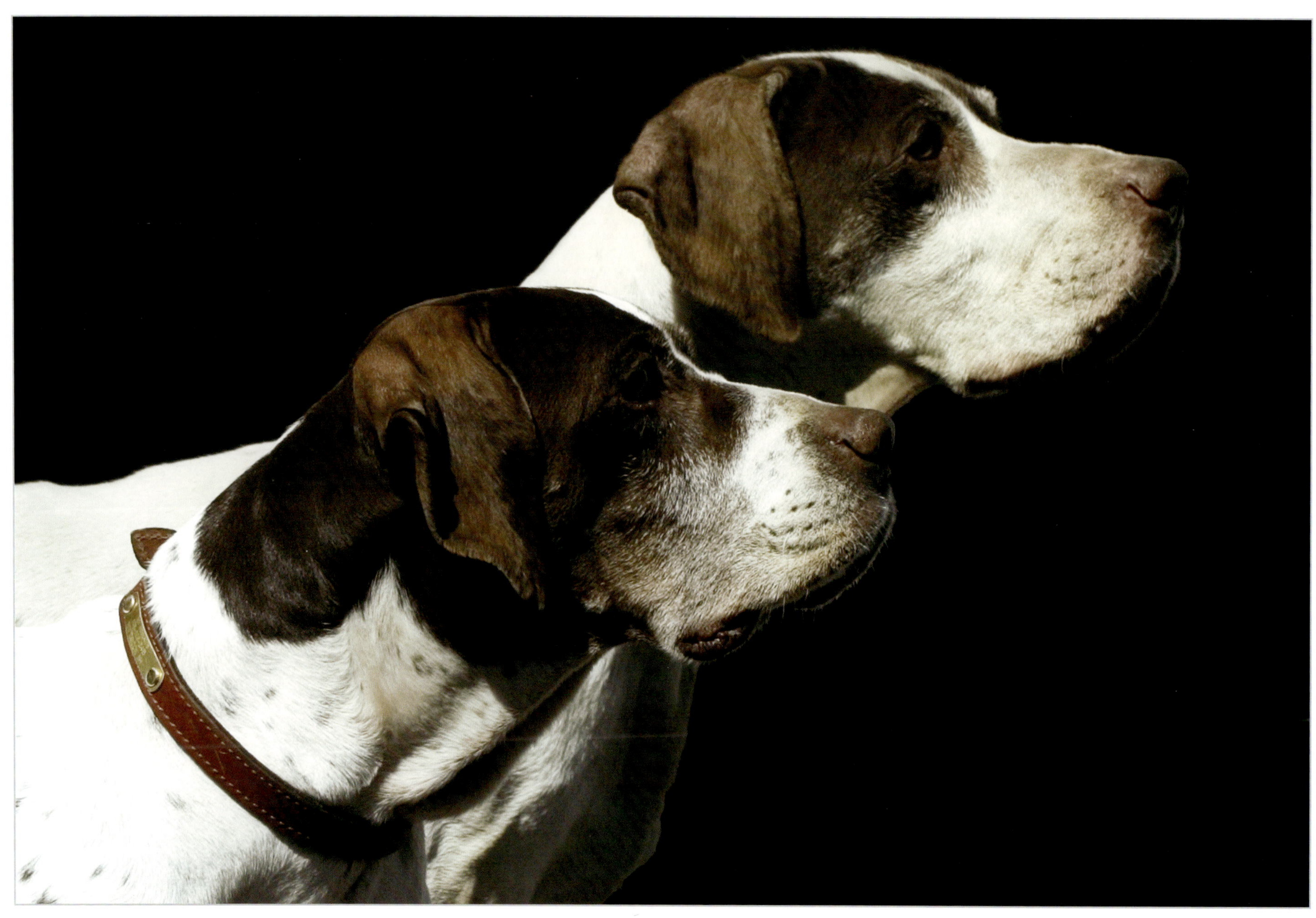

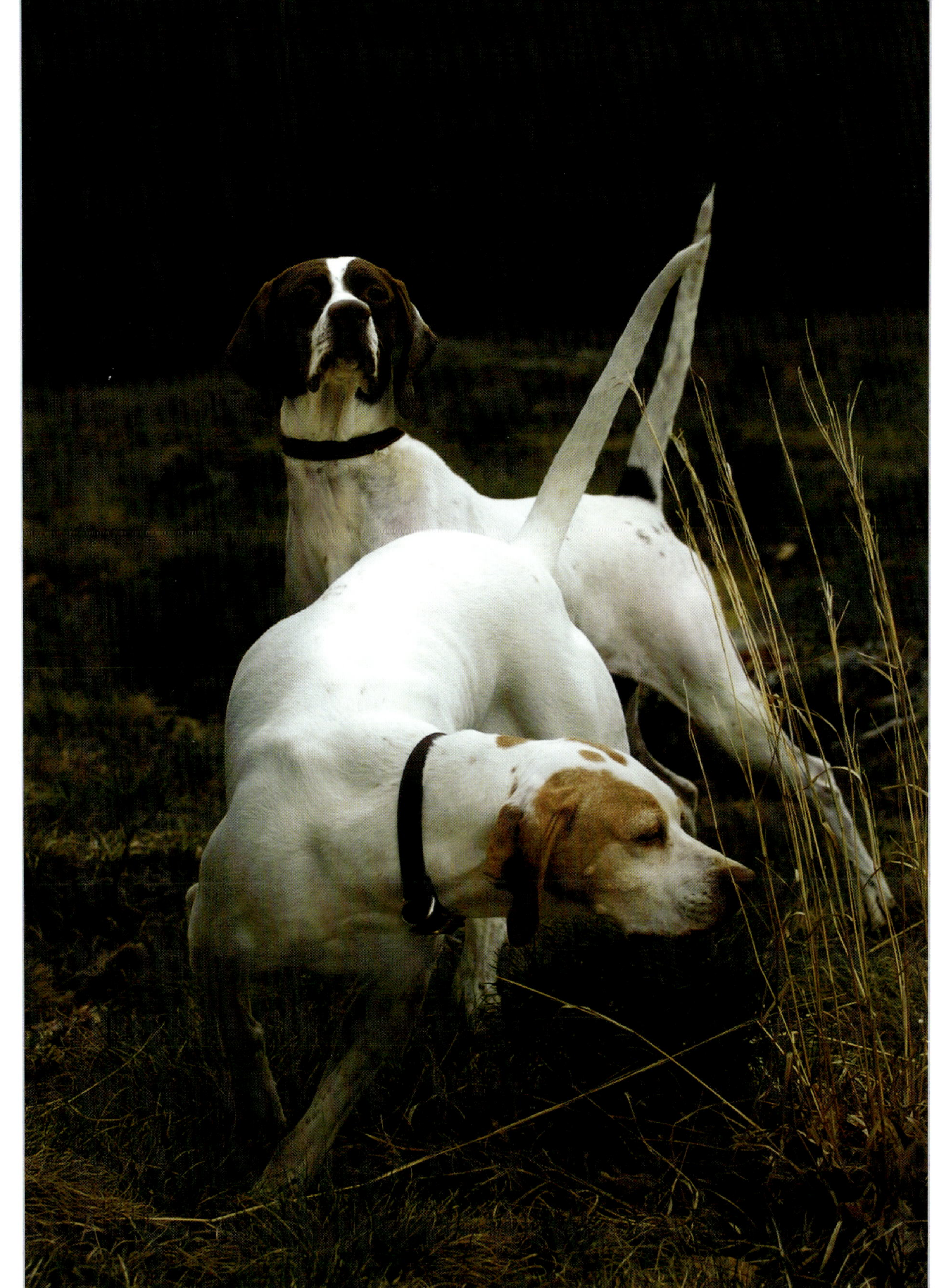

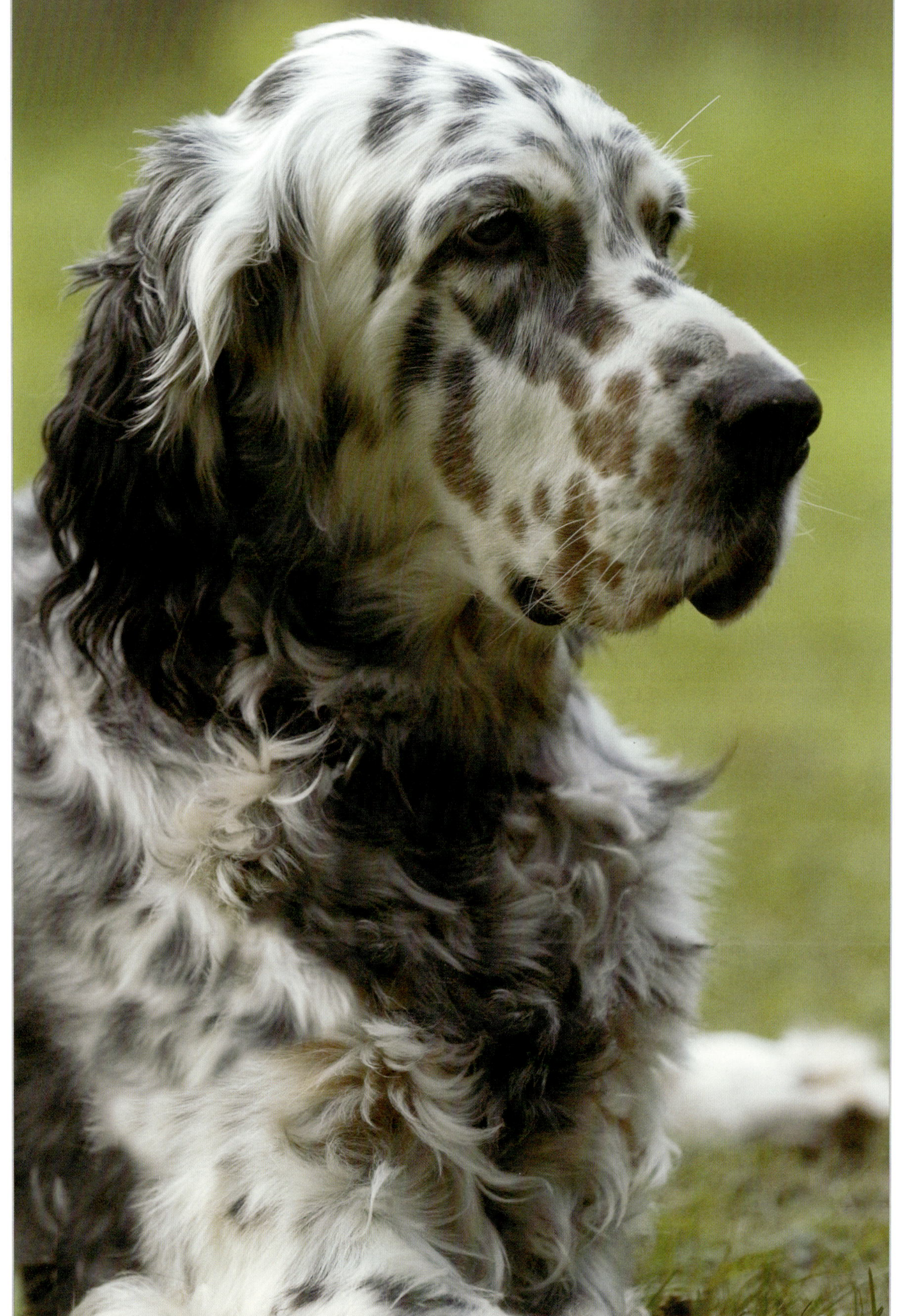

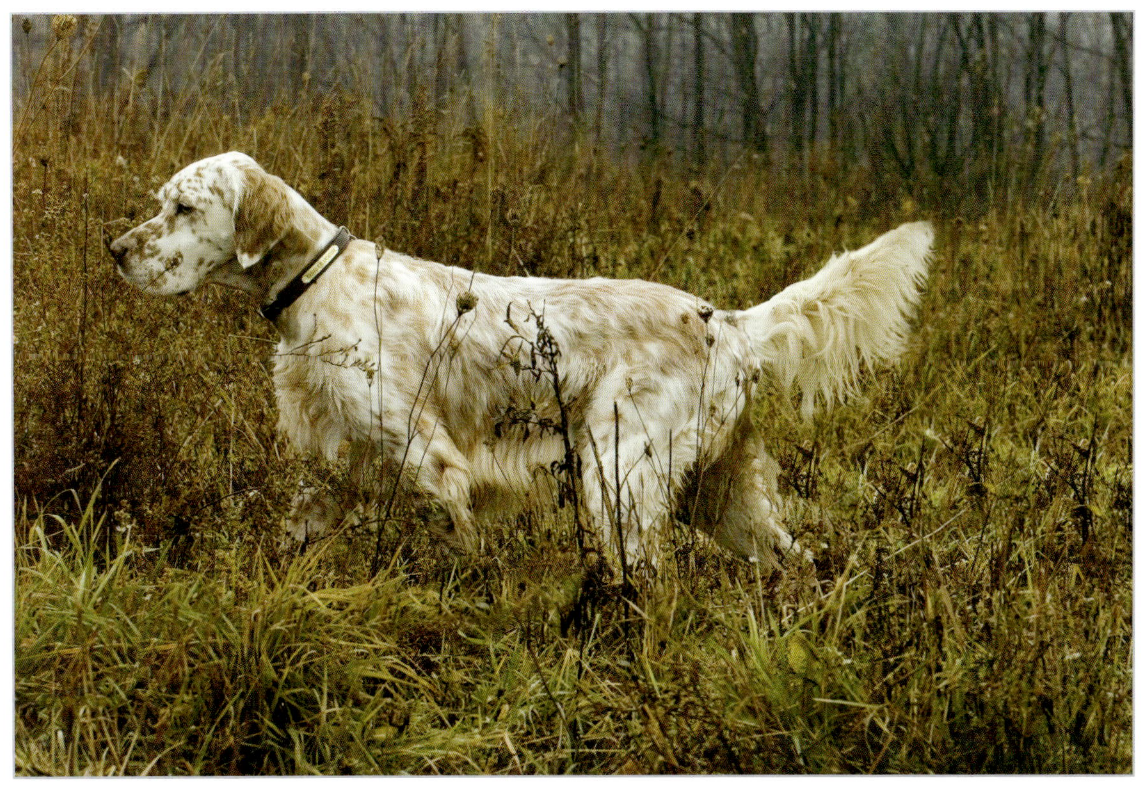

English setters are gentlemen by nature; they are of the best disposition without fear or viciousness, mild mannered, loving and devoted every moment of their lives, and a setter's eye is one of the jewels of the entire animal kingdom. ~Captain Will Judy

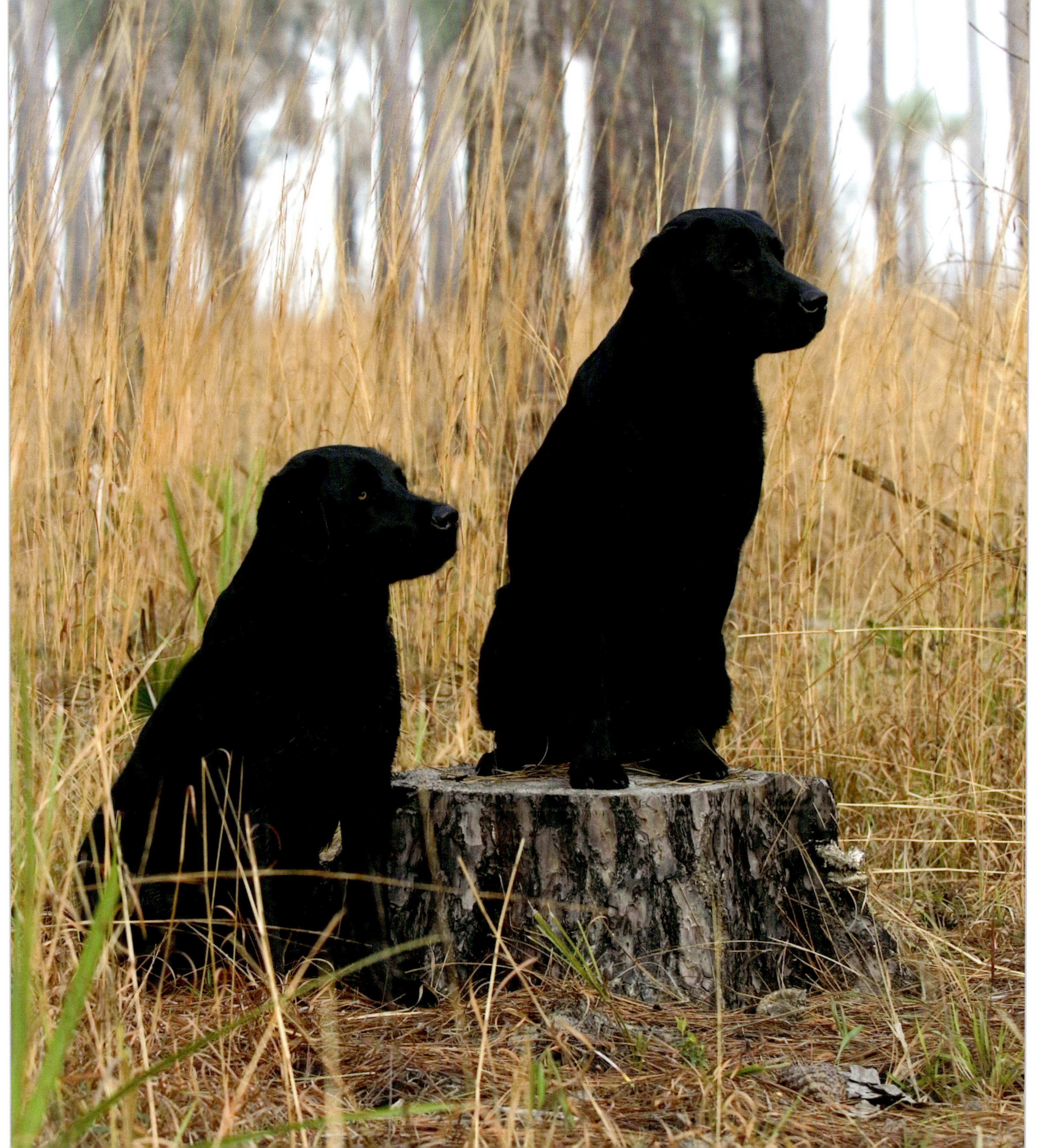

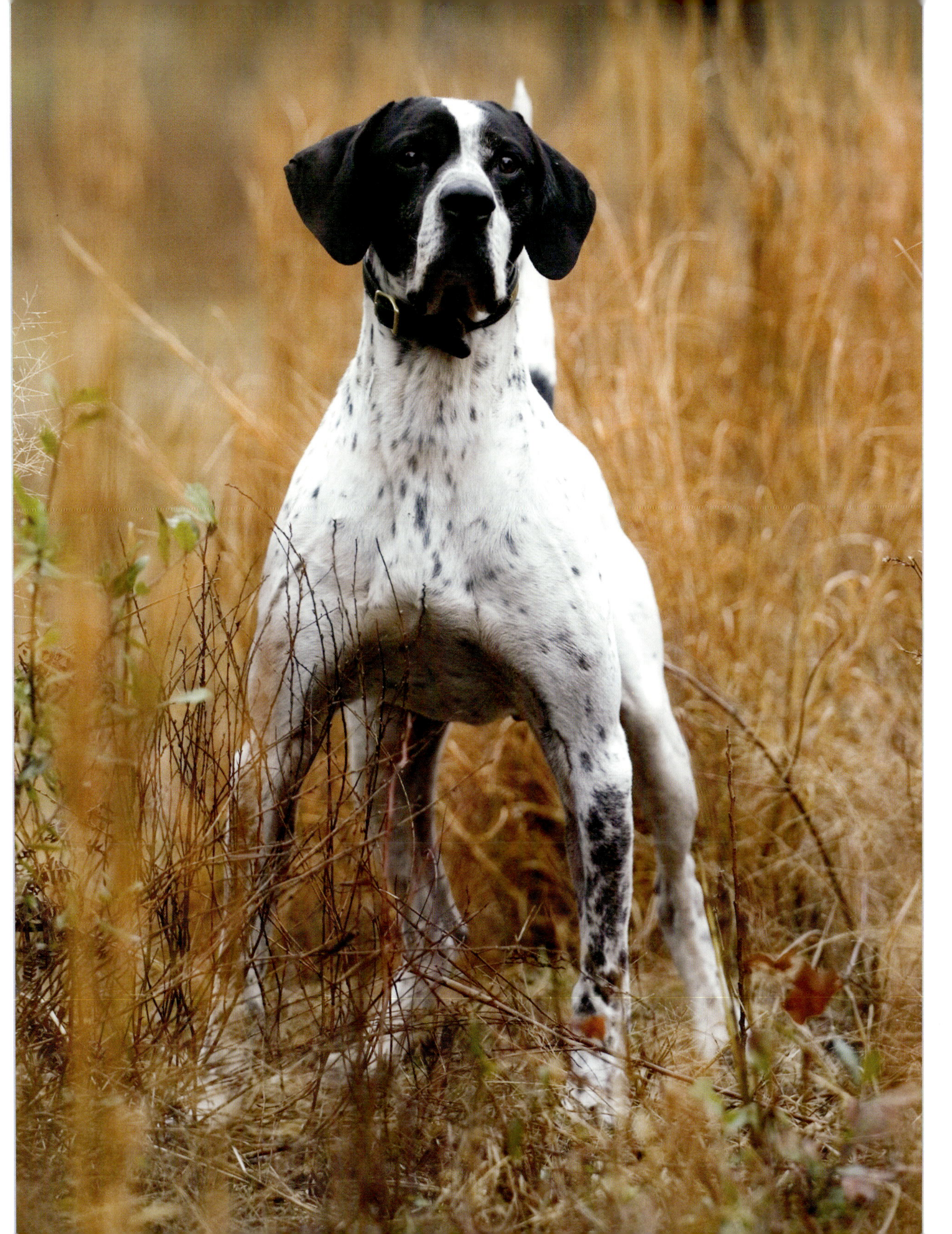

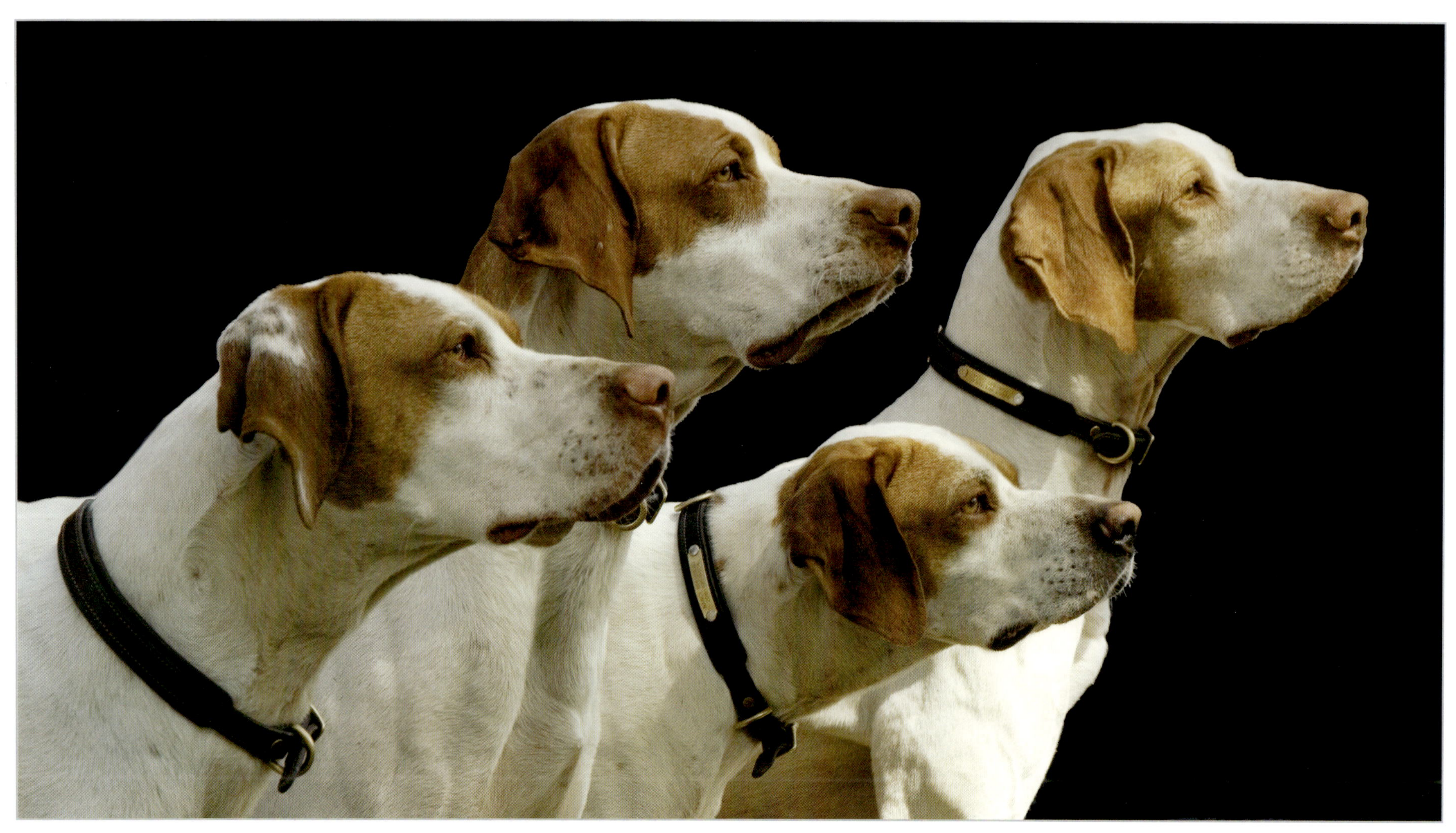

A thing of beauty is a joy forever. ~John Keats

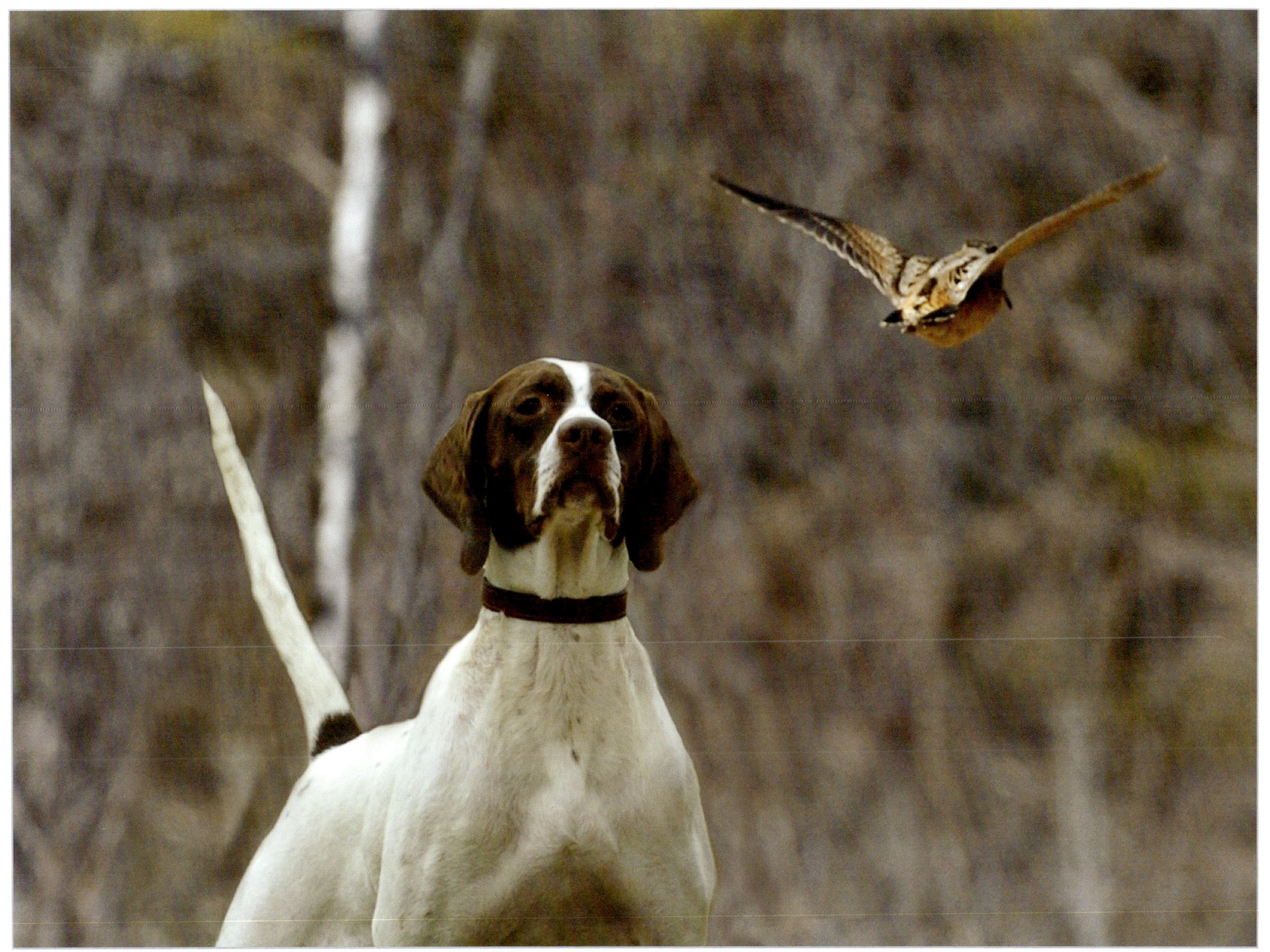

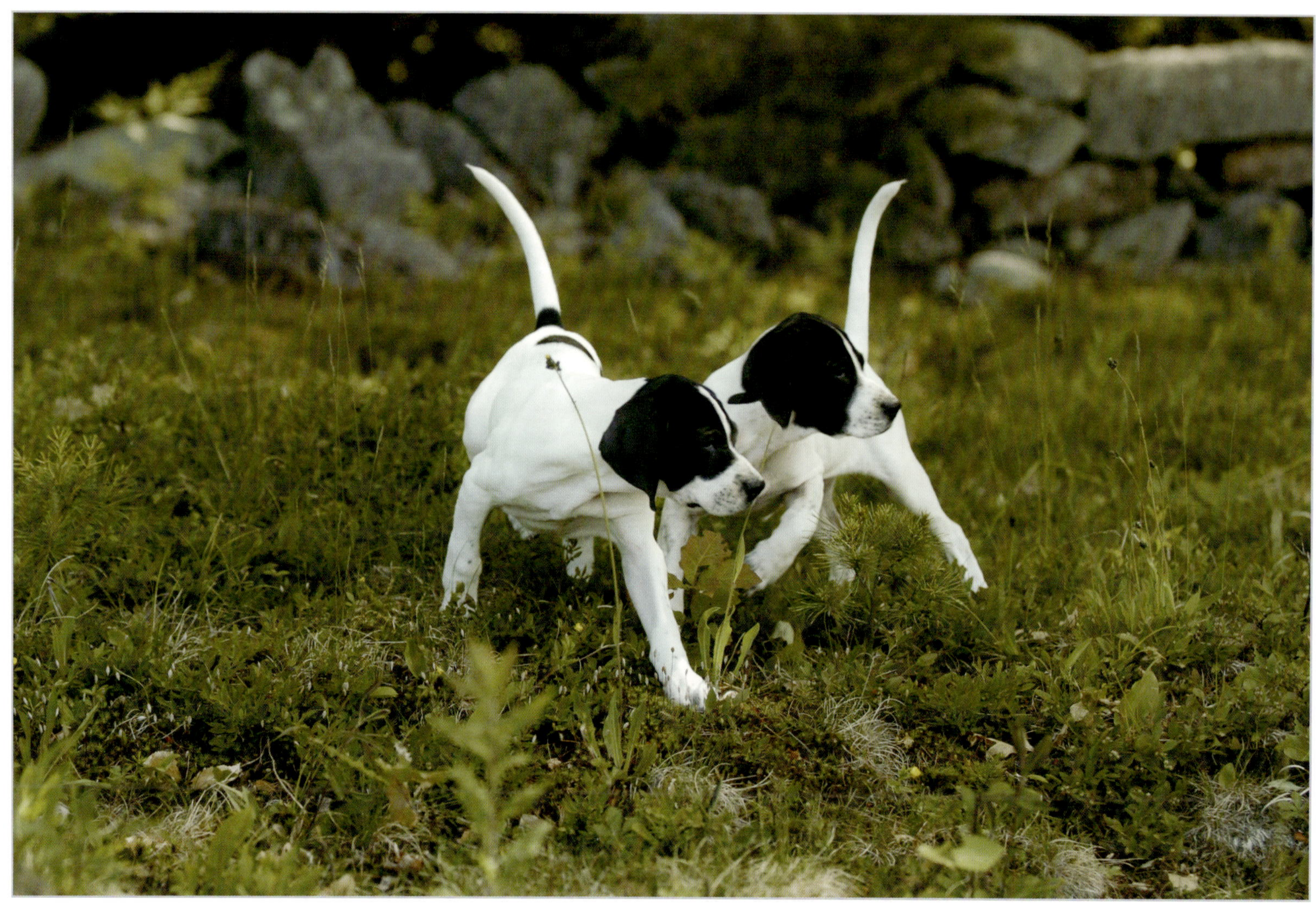

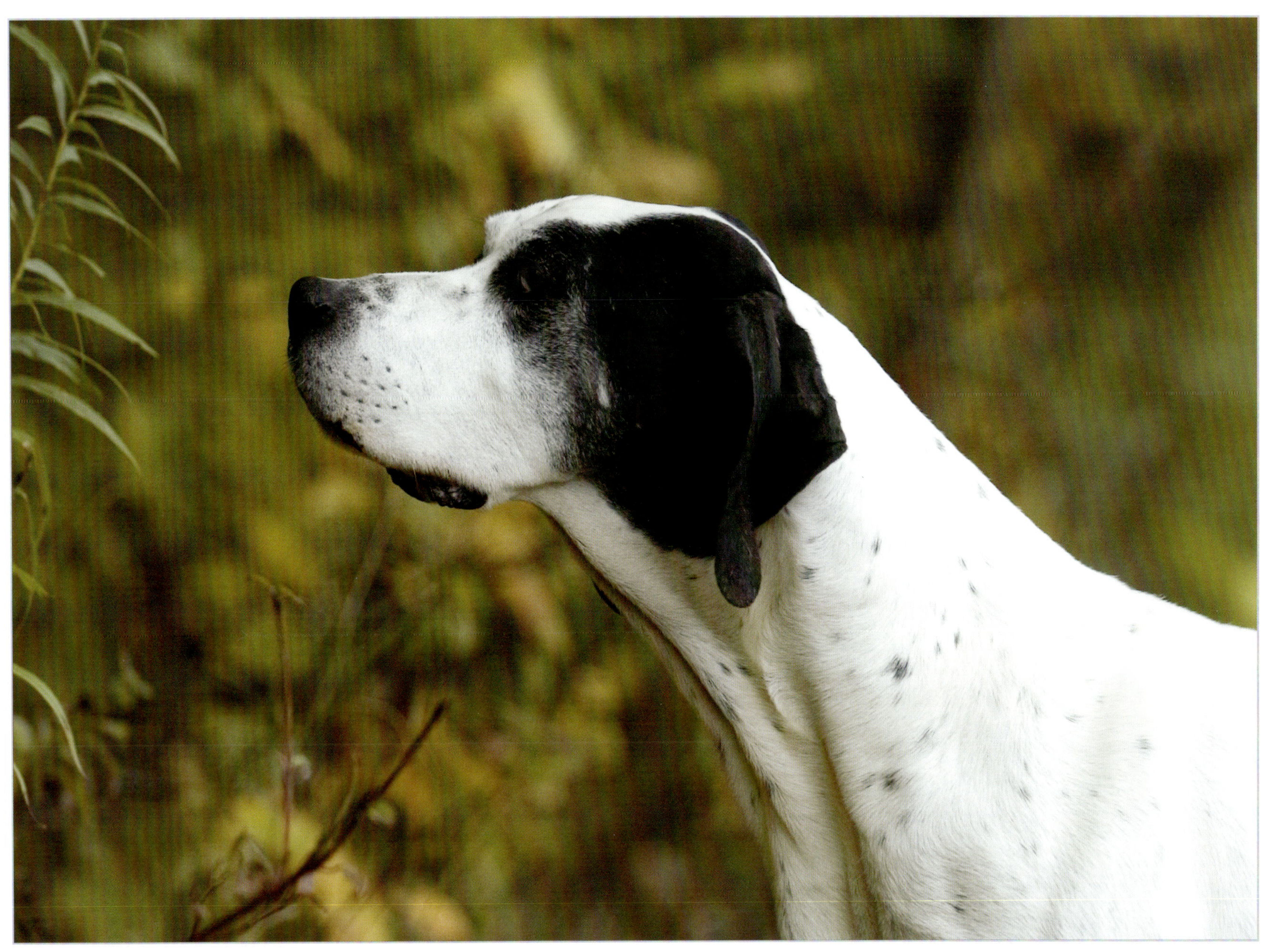

Never deny a sporting dog what he or she was bred for, what they live for. ~C.E. Metz

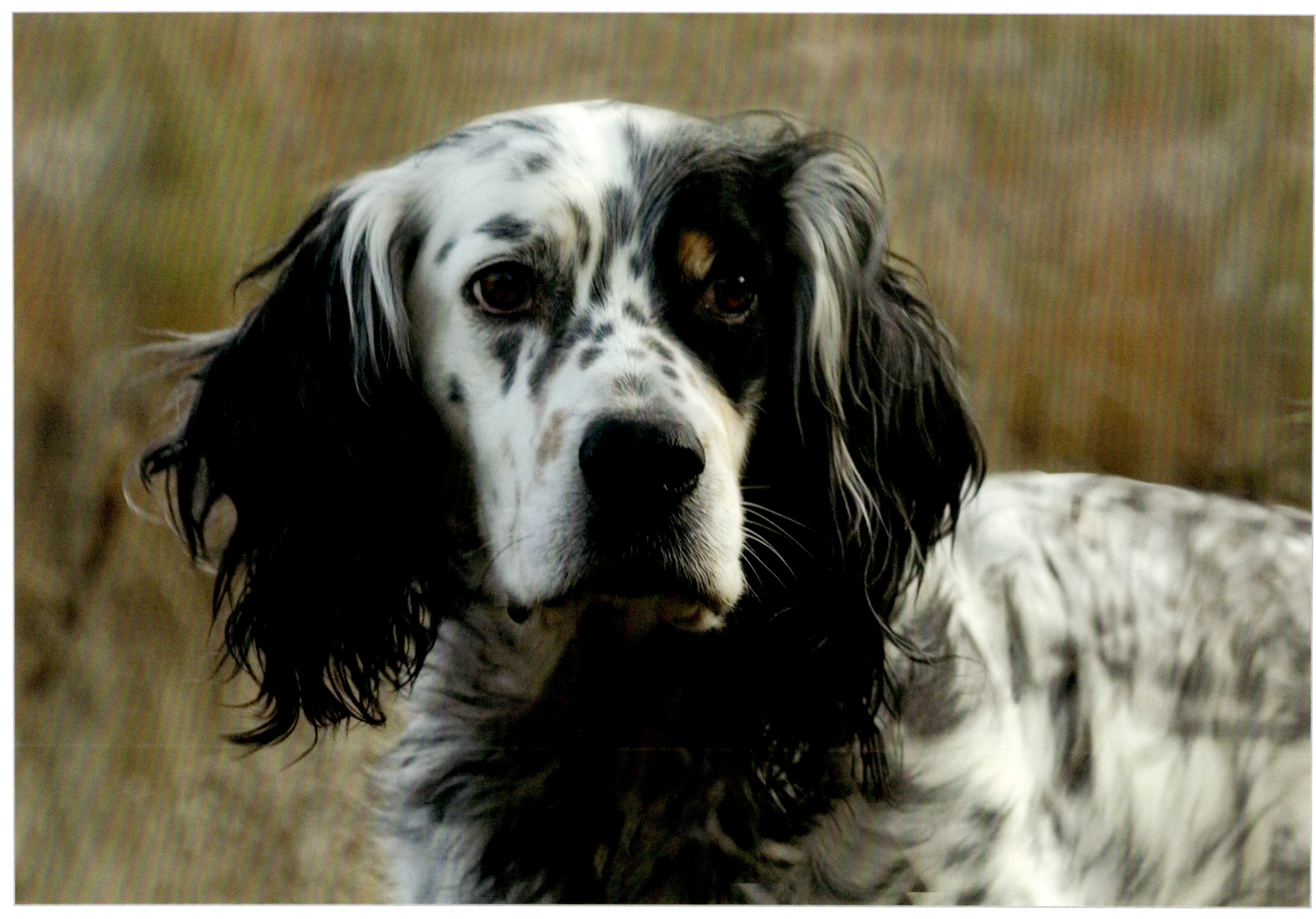

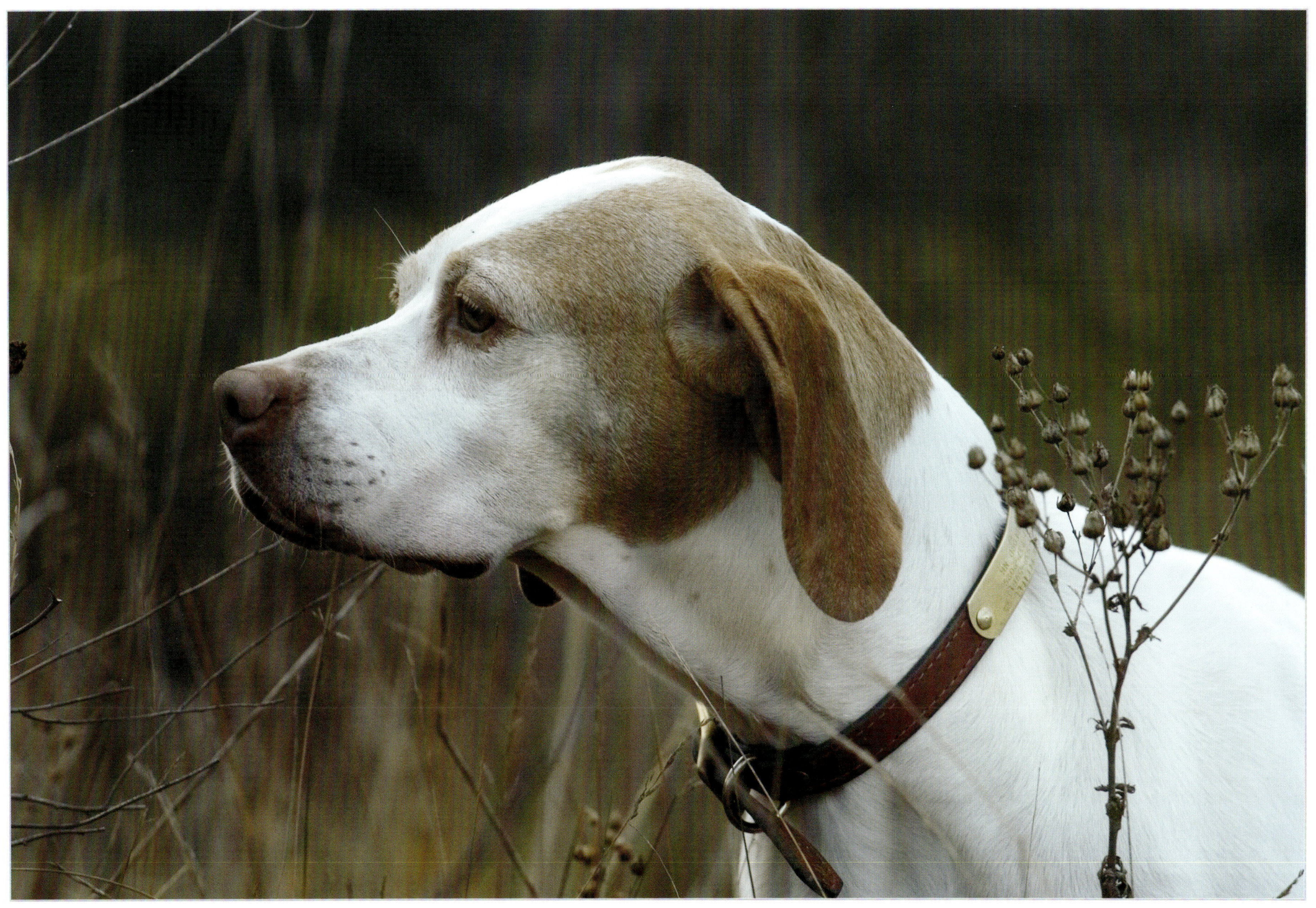

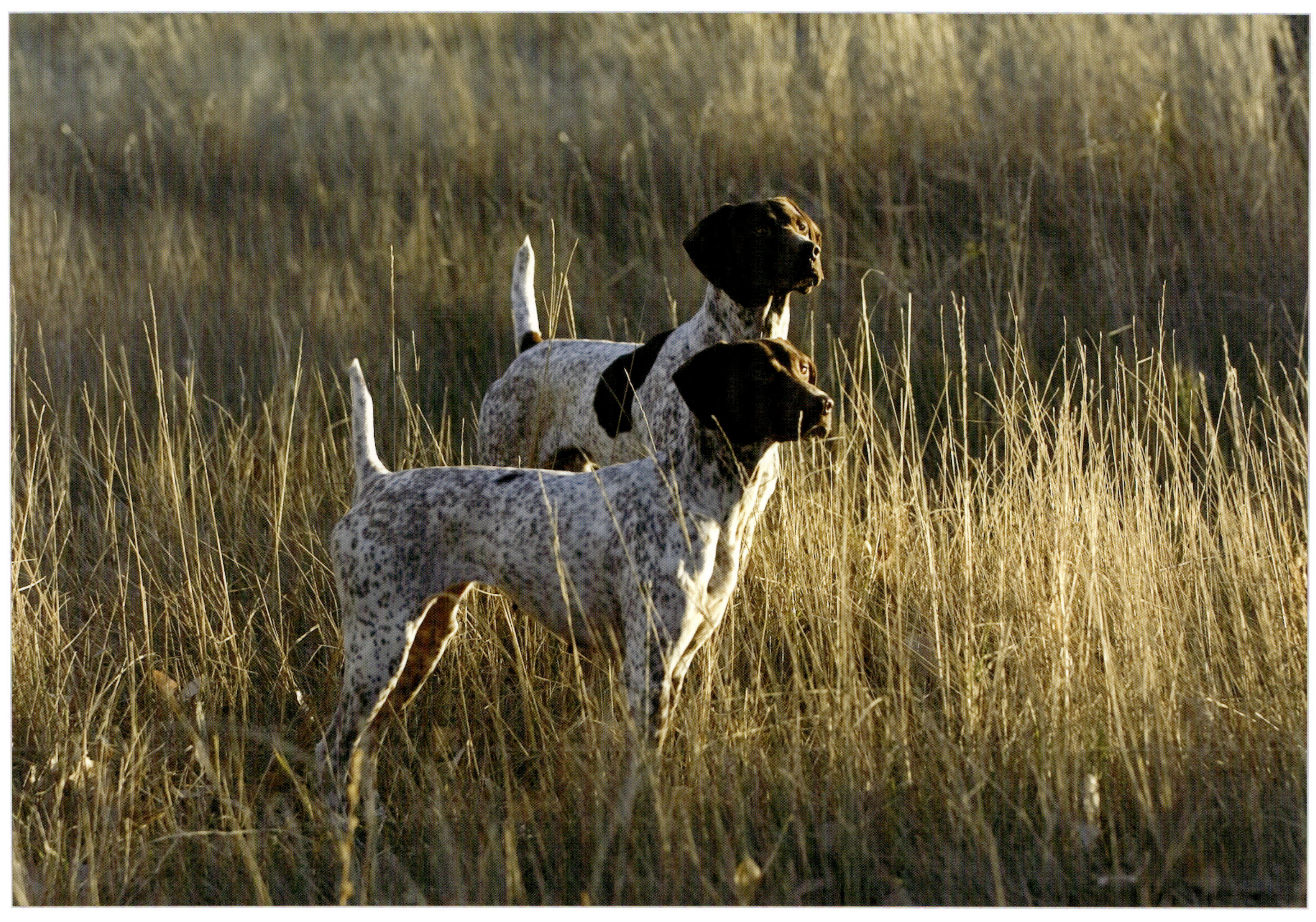

Dogs are not our whole life, but they make our lives whole. ~Robert Caras

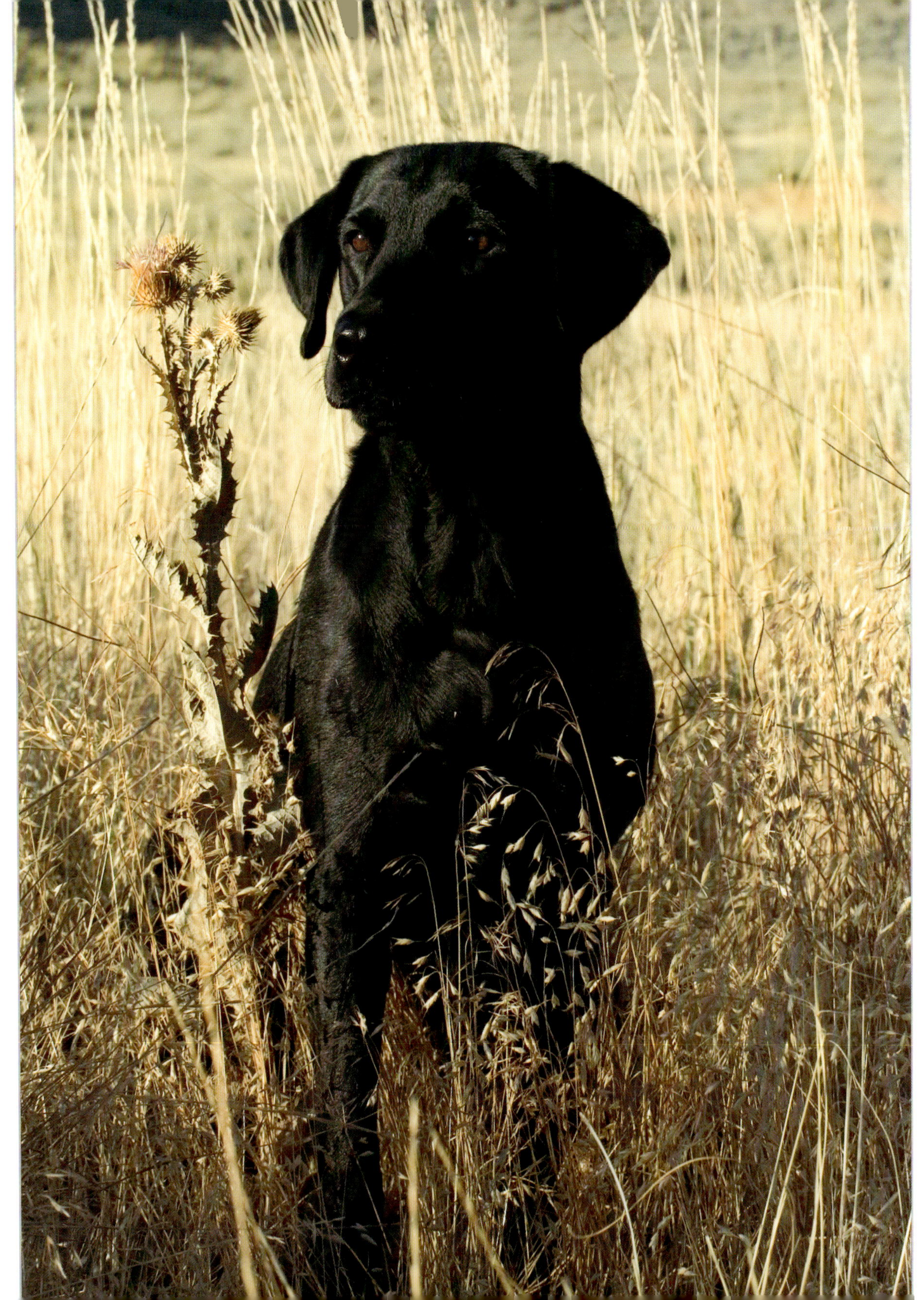

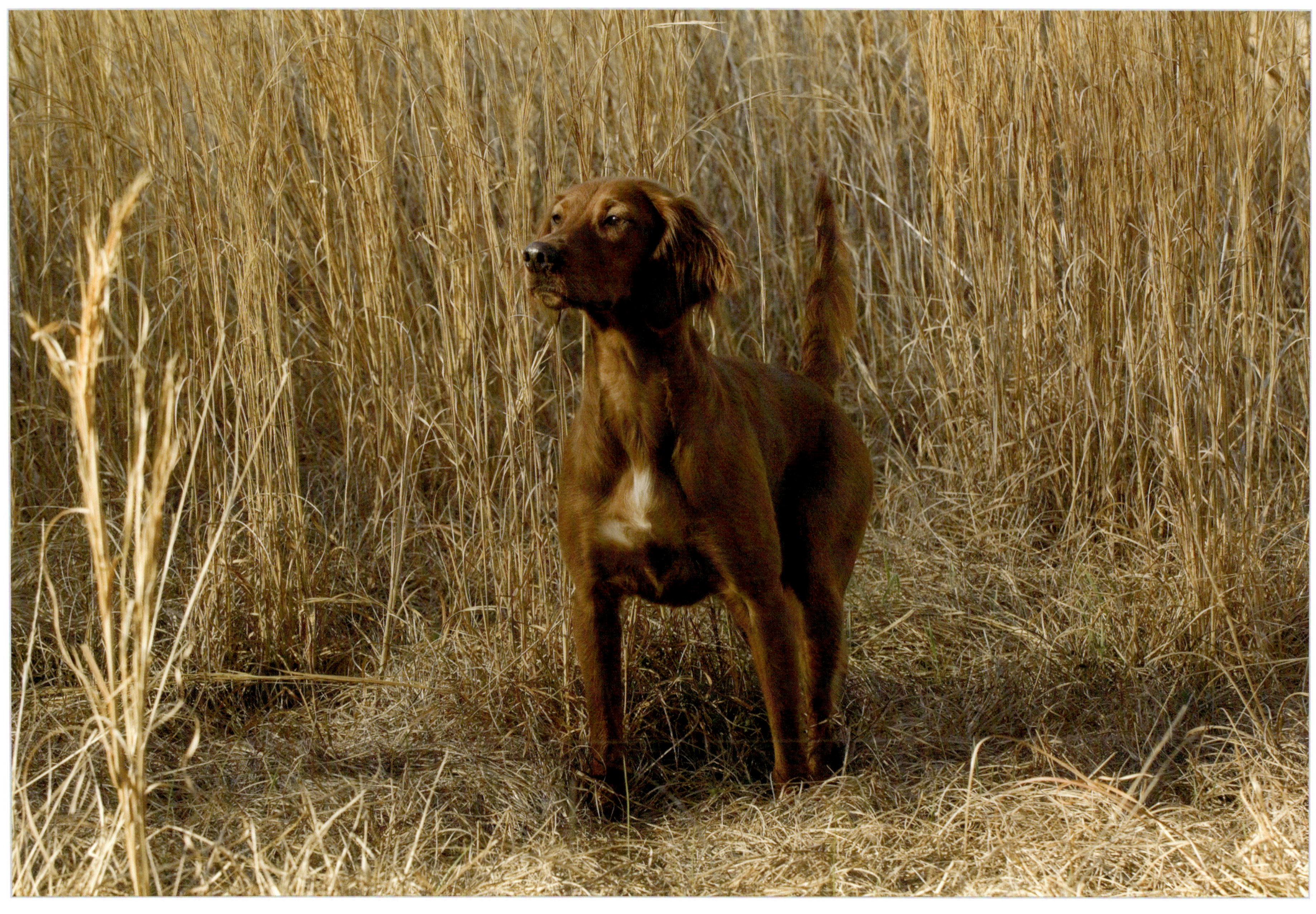

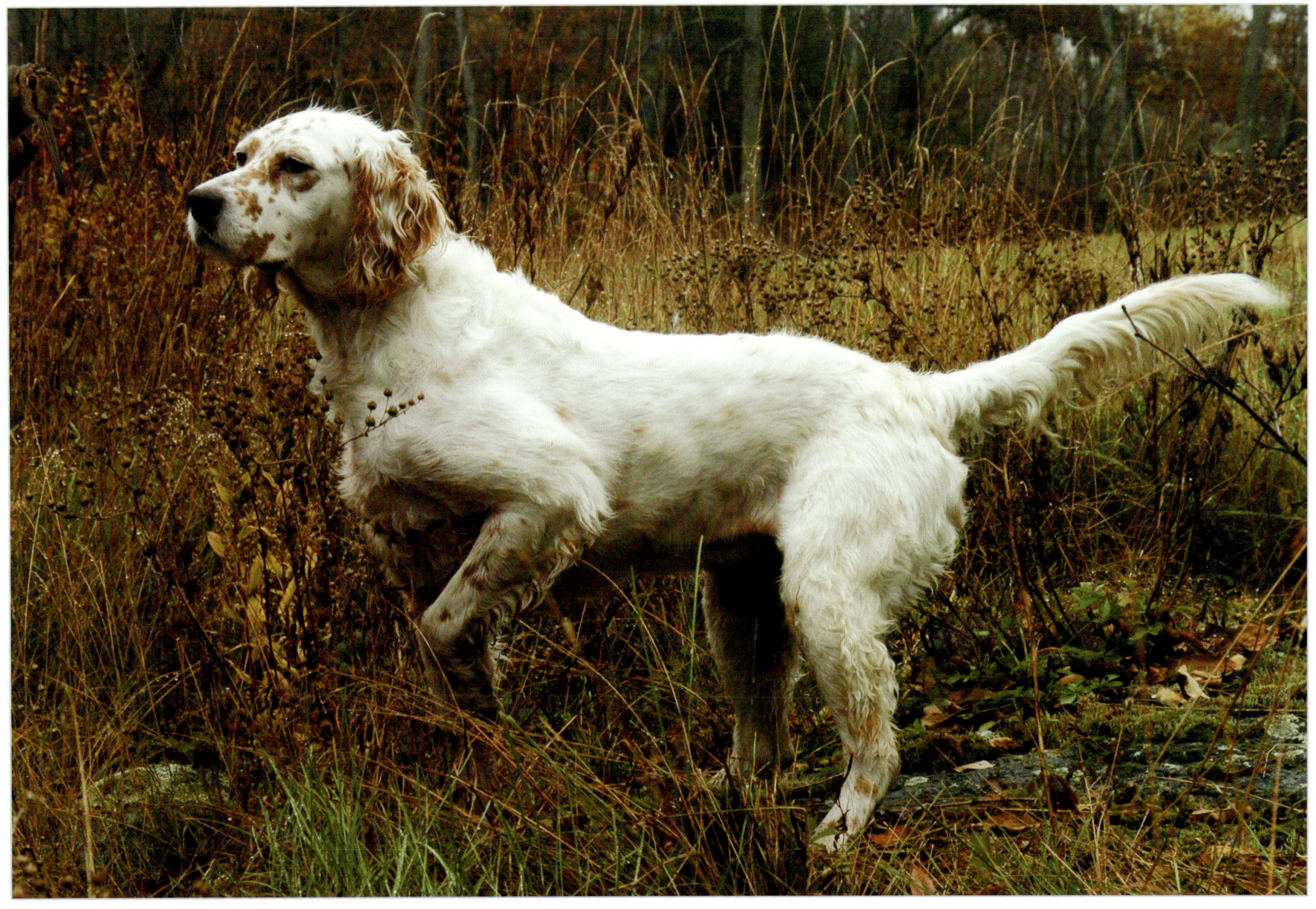

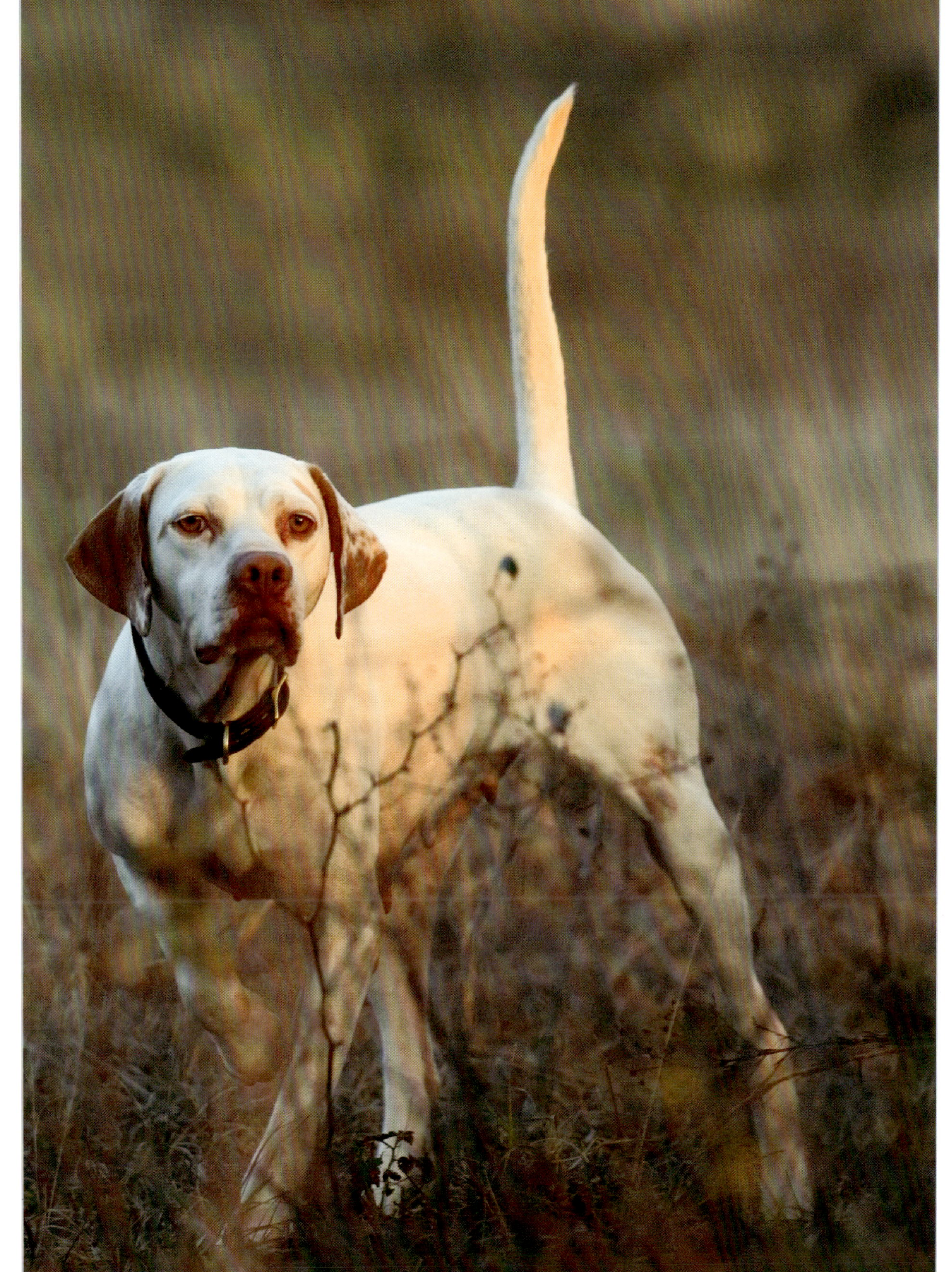

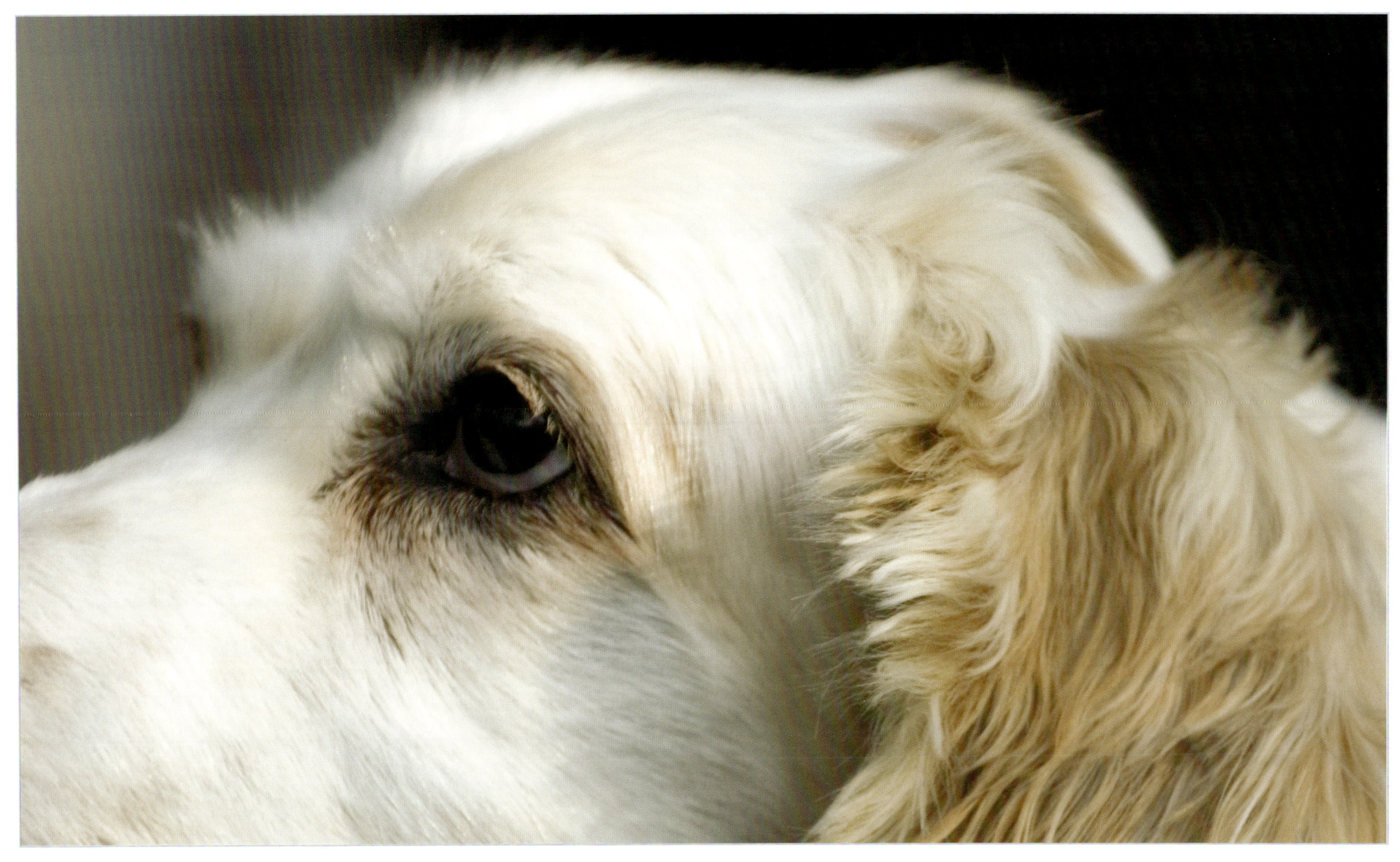

Could a greater miracle take place than for us to look through each other's eyes for an instant? ~Henry David Thoreau

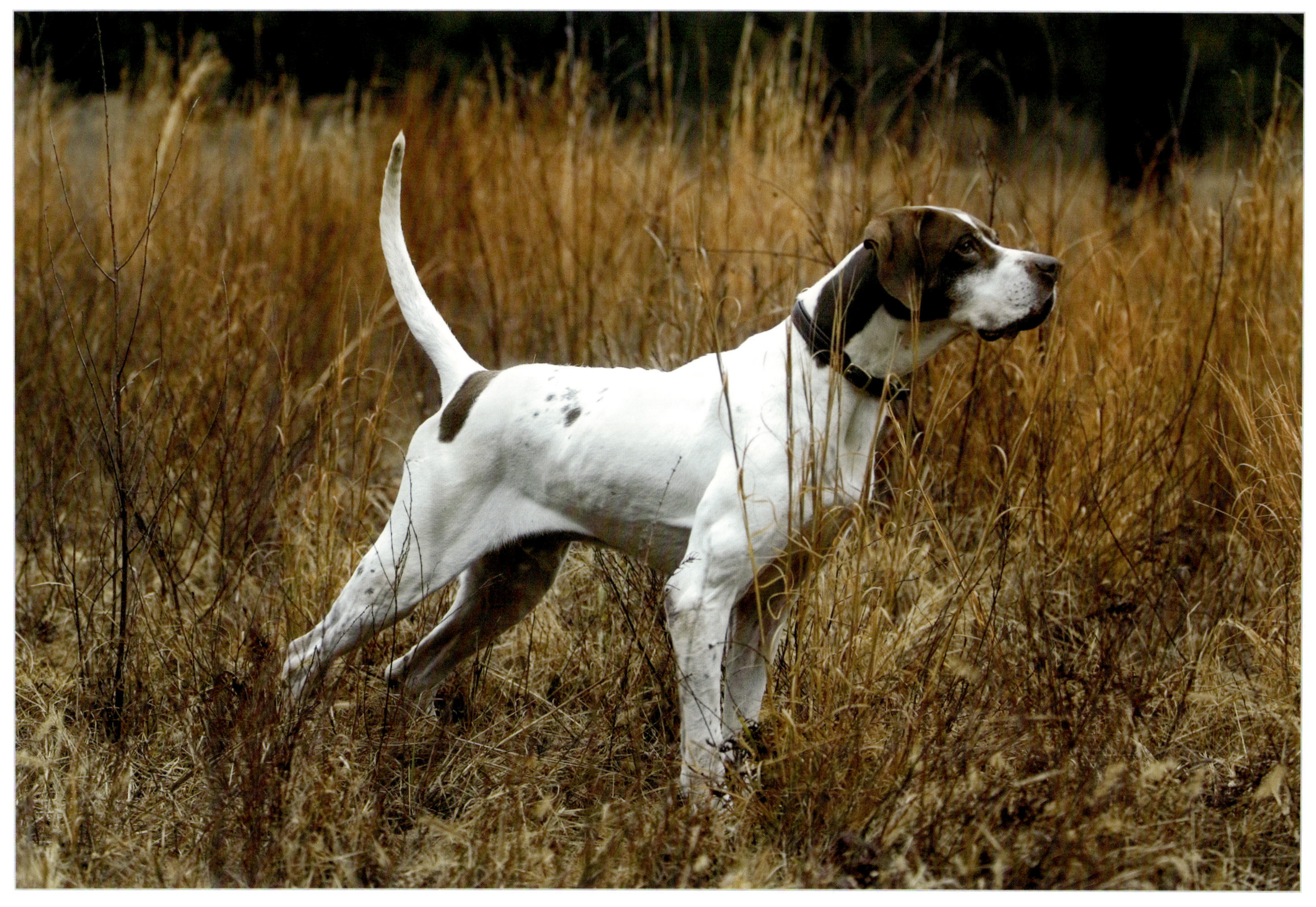

A picture is worth a thousand points. ~C.E. Metz

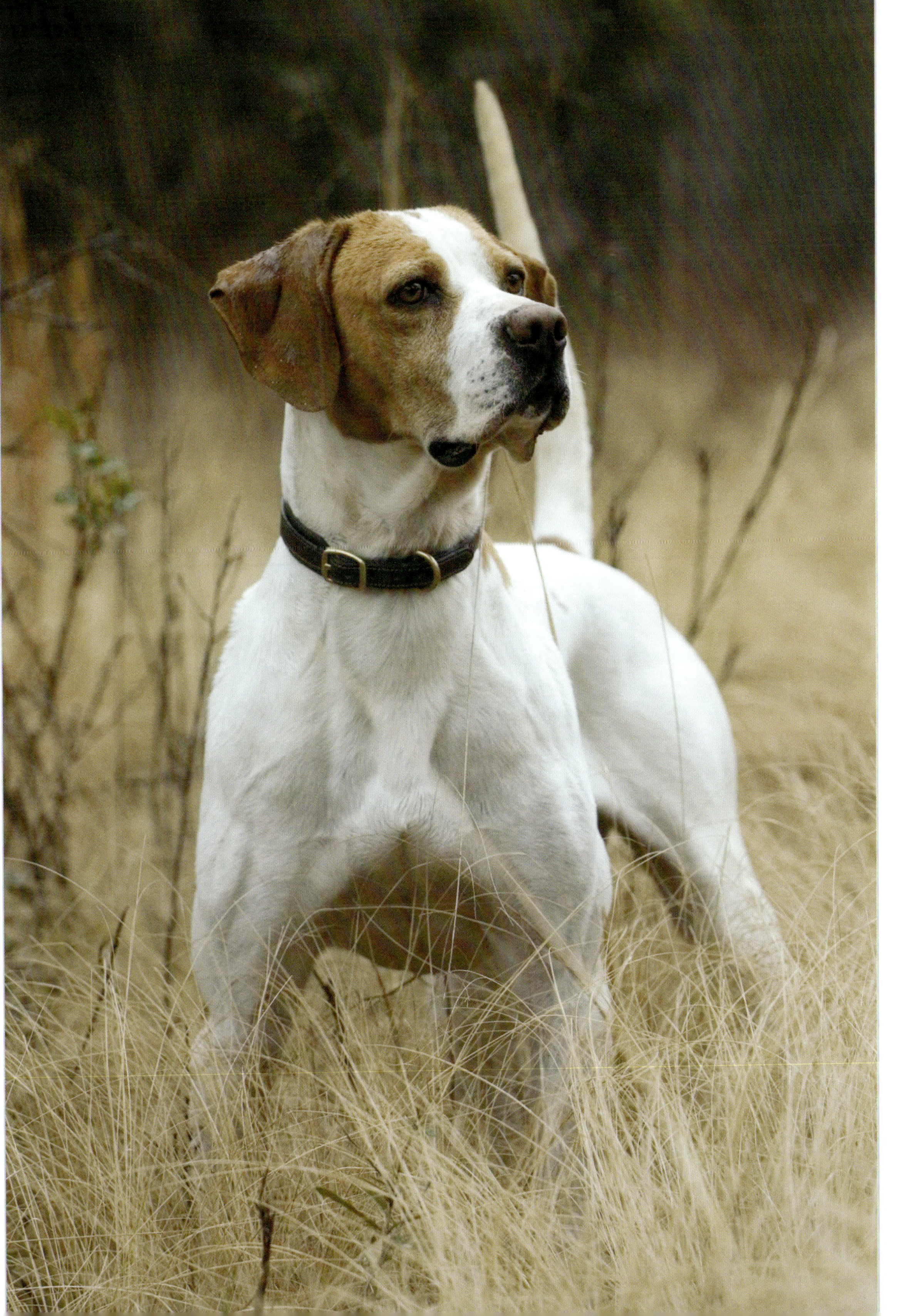

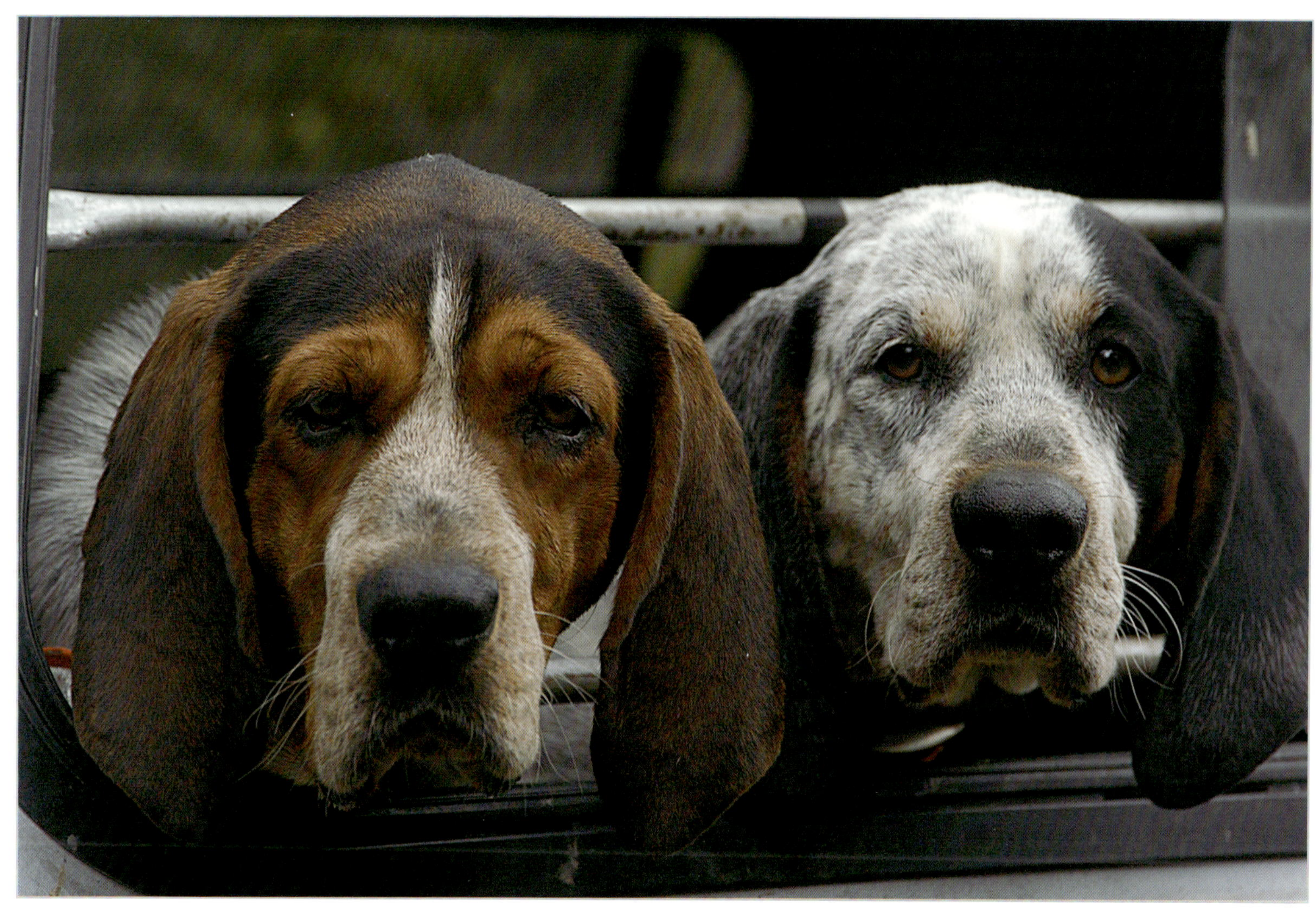

Those who have never been owned by a sporting dog have missed one of life's greatest pleasures. ~C.E. Metz

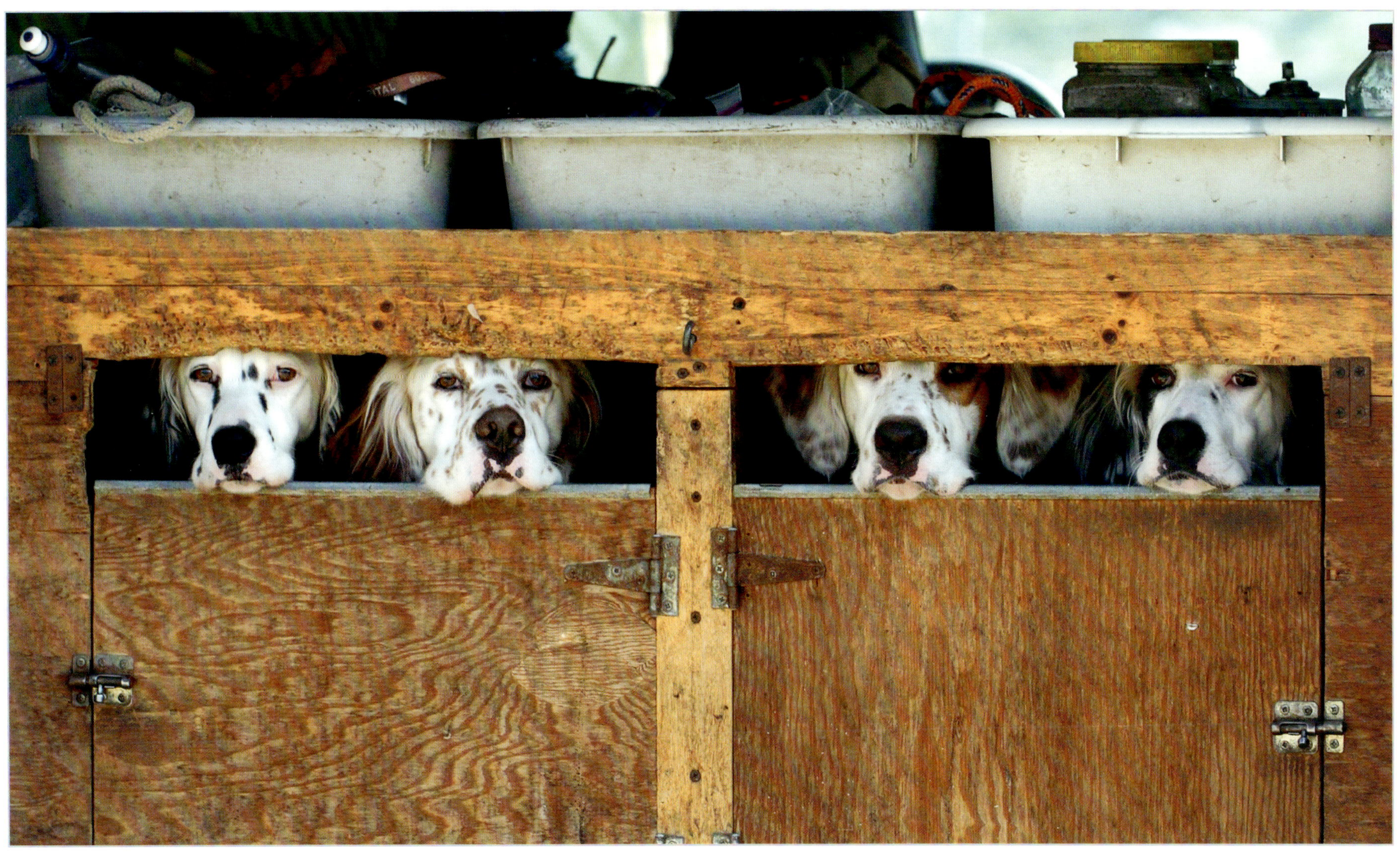

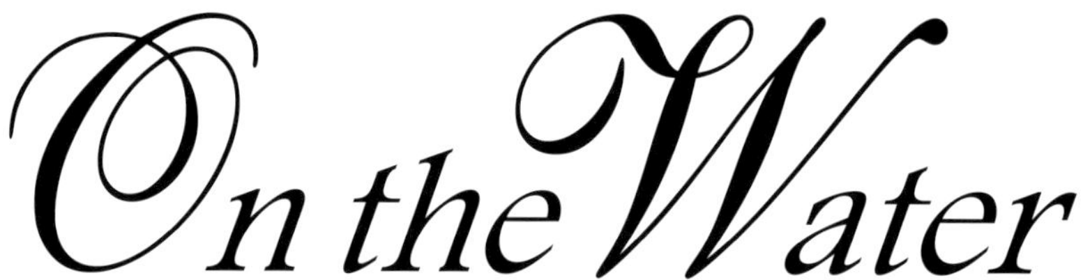

You ask of my companions. Hills, sir, and the sundown and a dog as large as myself that my father bought me. They are better than human beings because they know but do not tell. ~Emily Dickinson

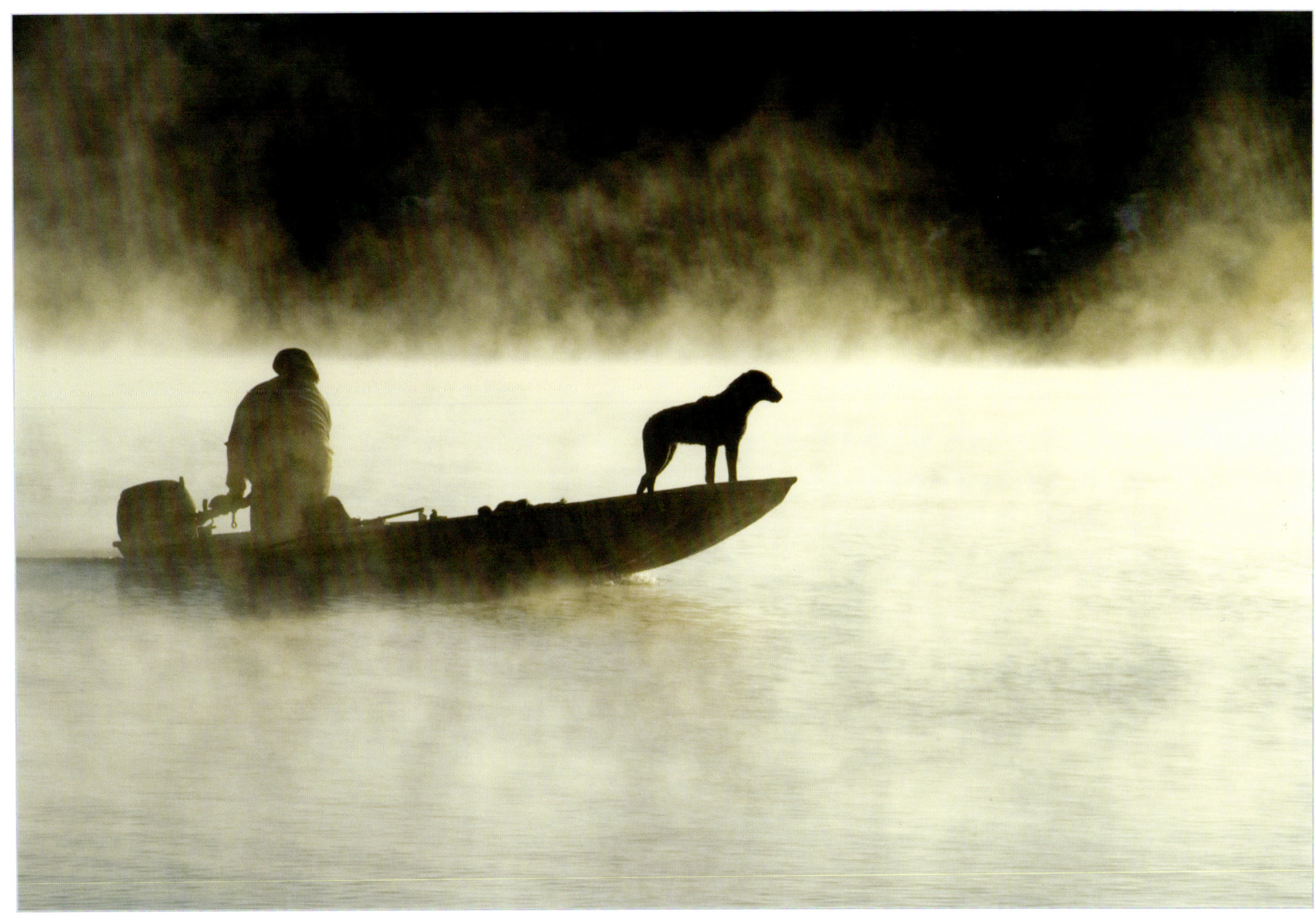

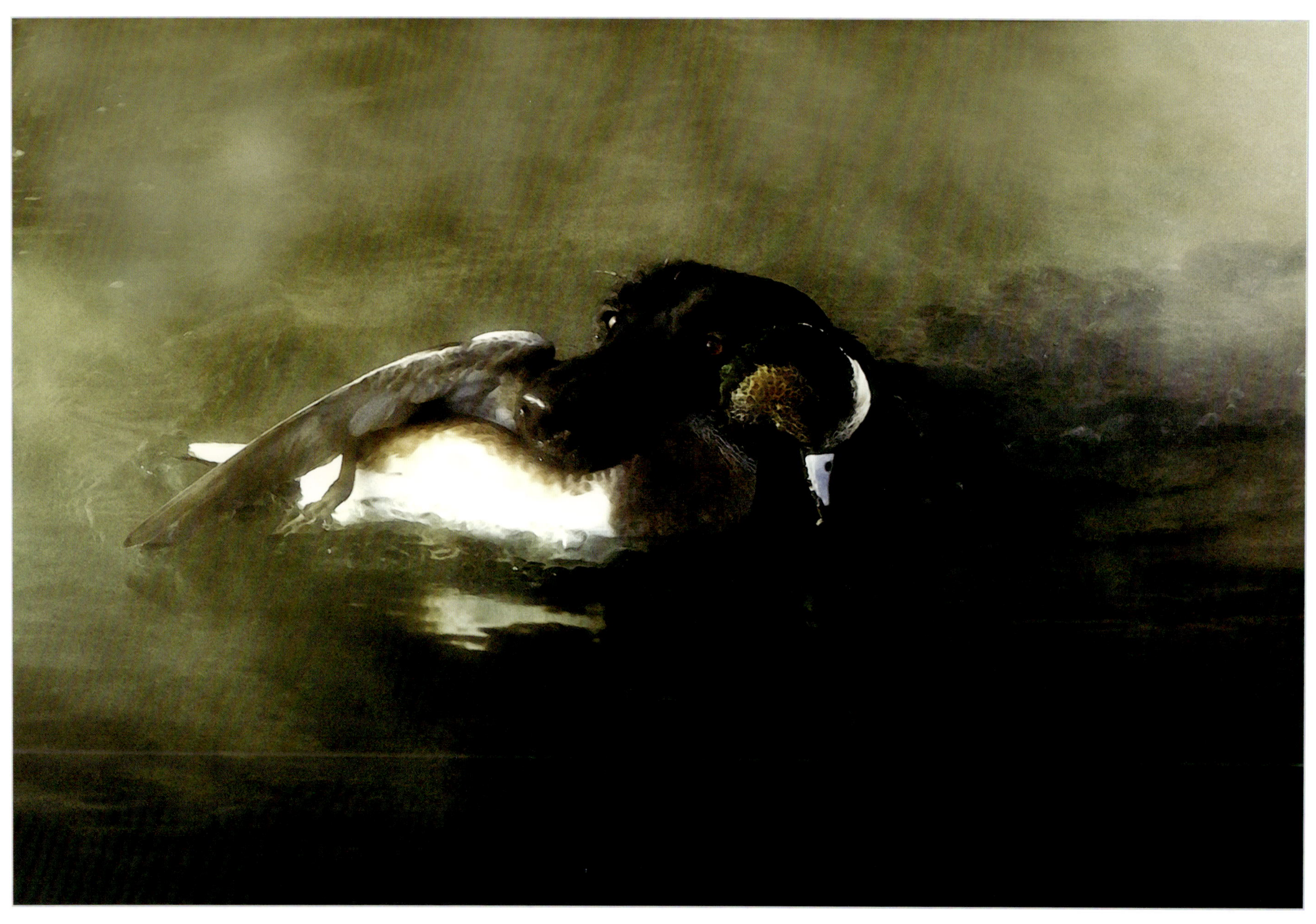

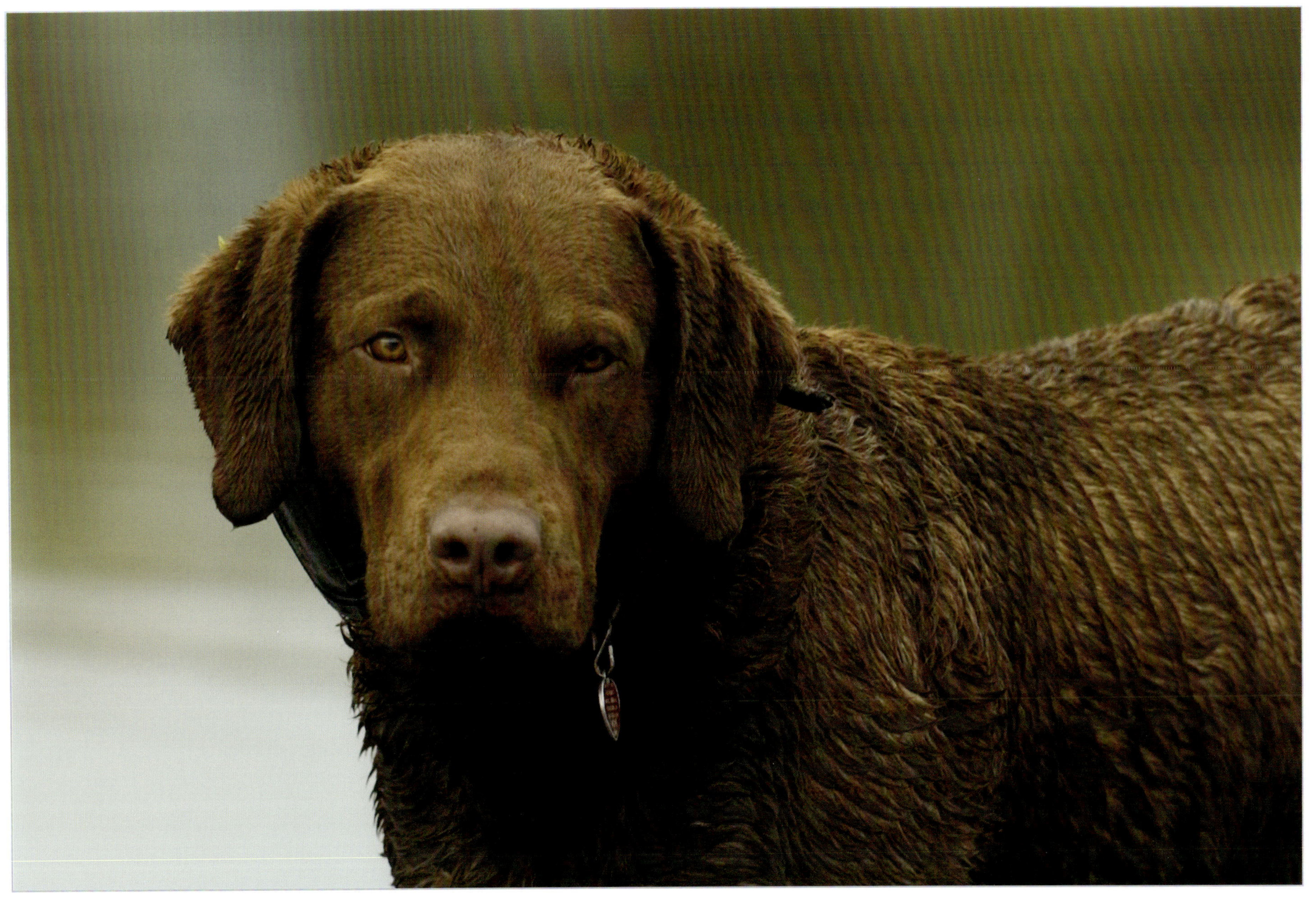

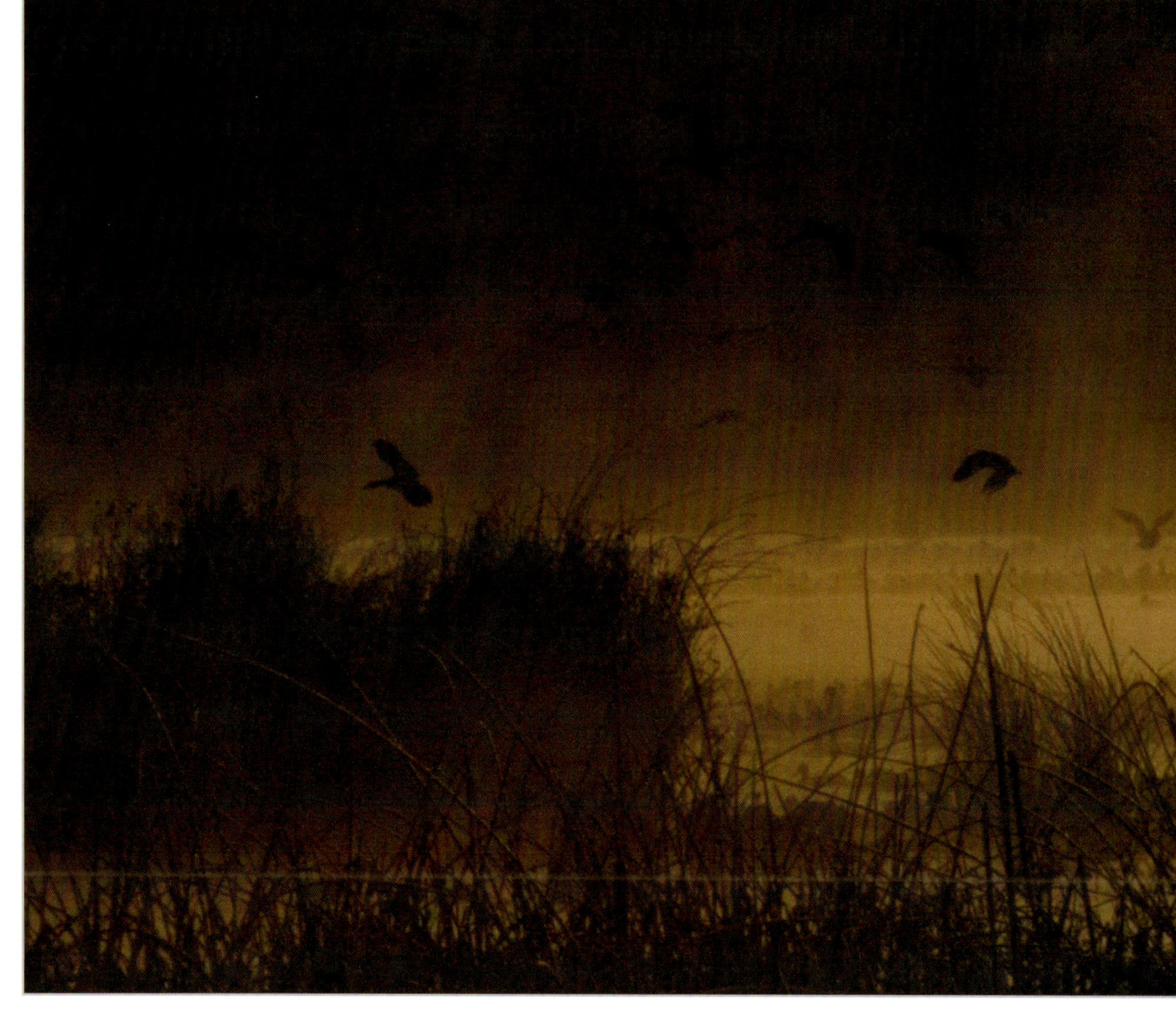

The color of water-the sound of wings.
~C.E. Metz

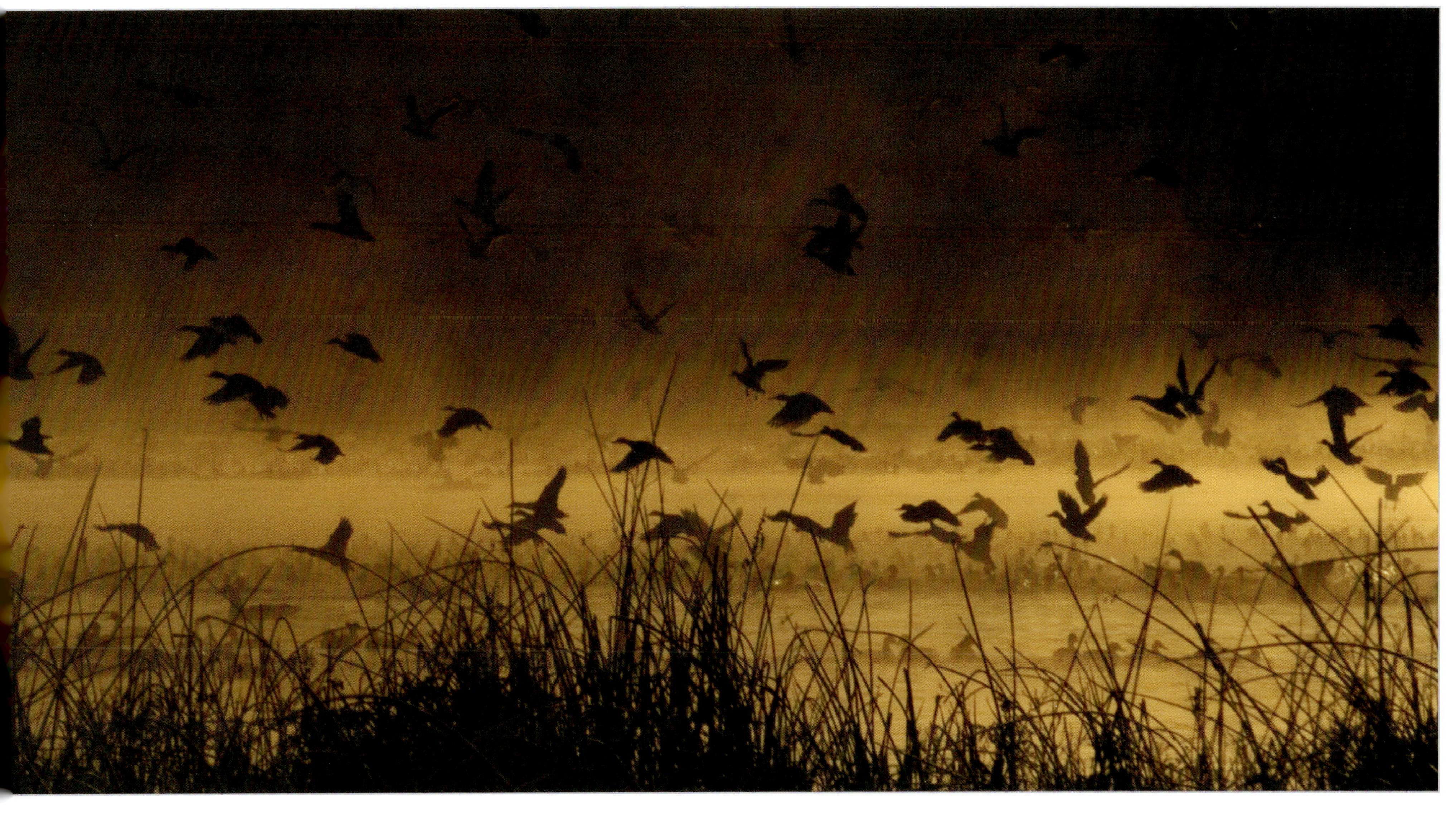

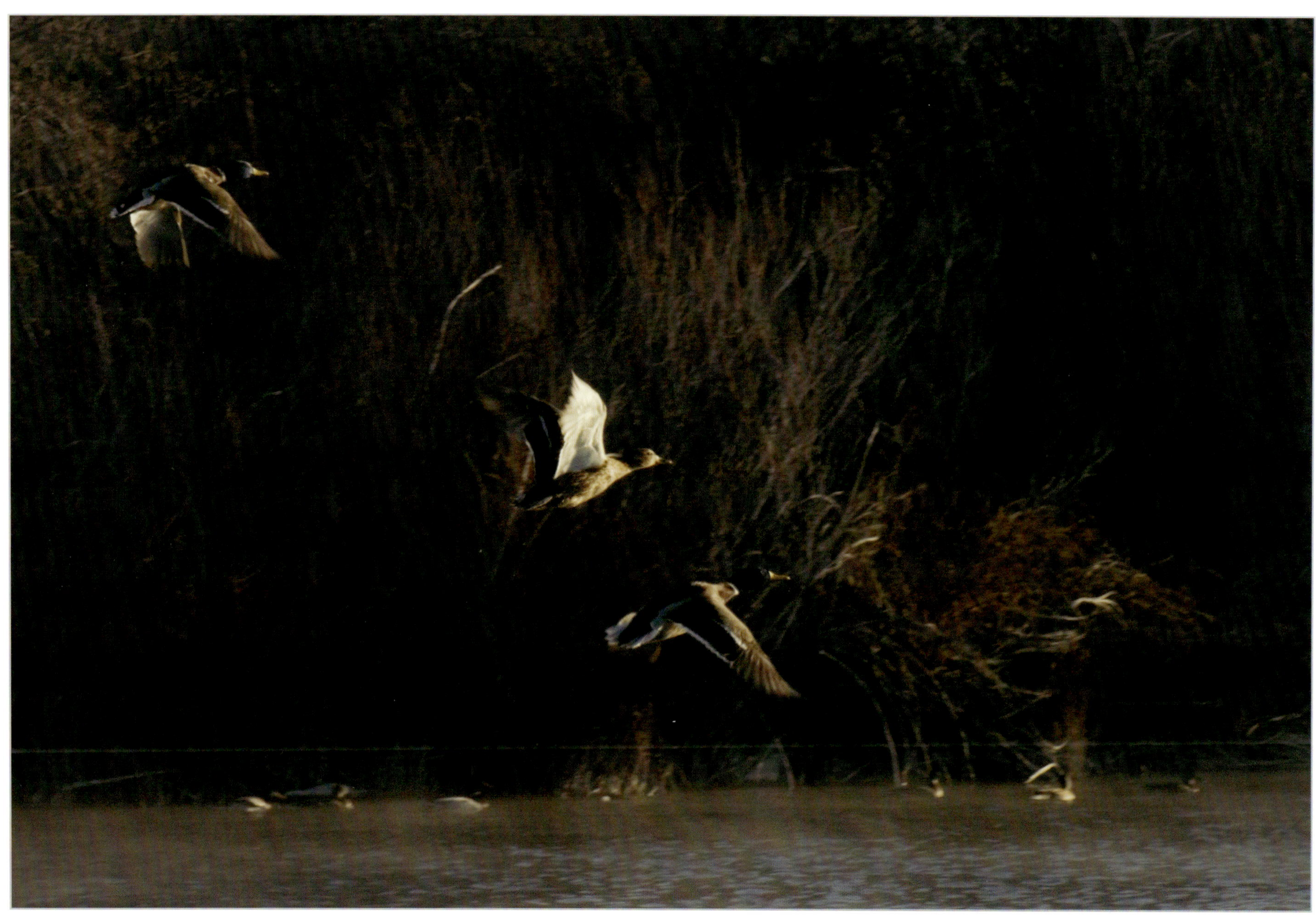

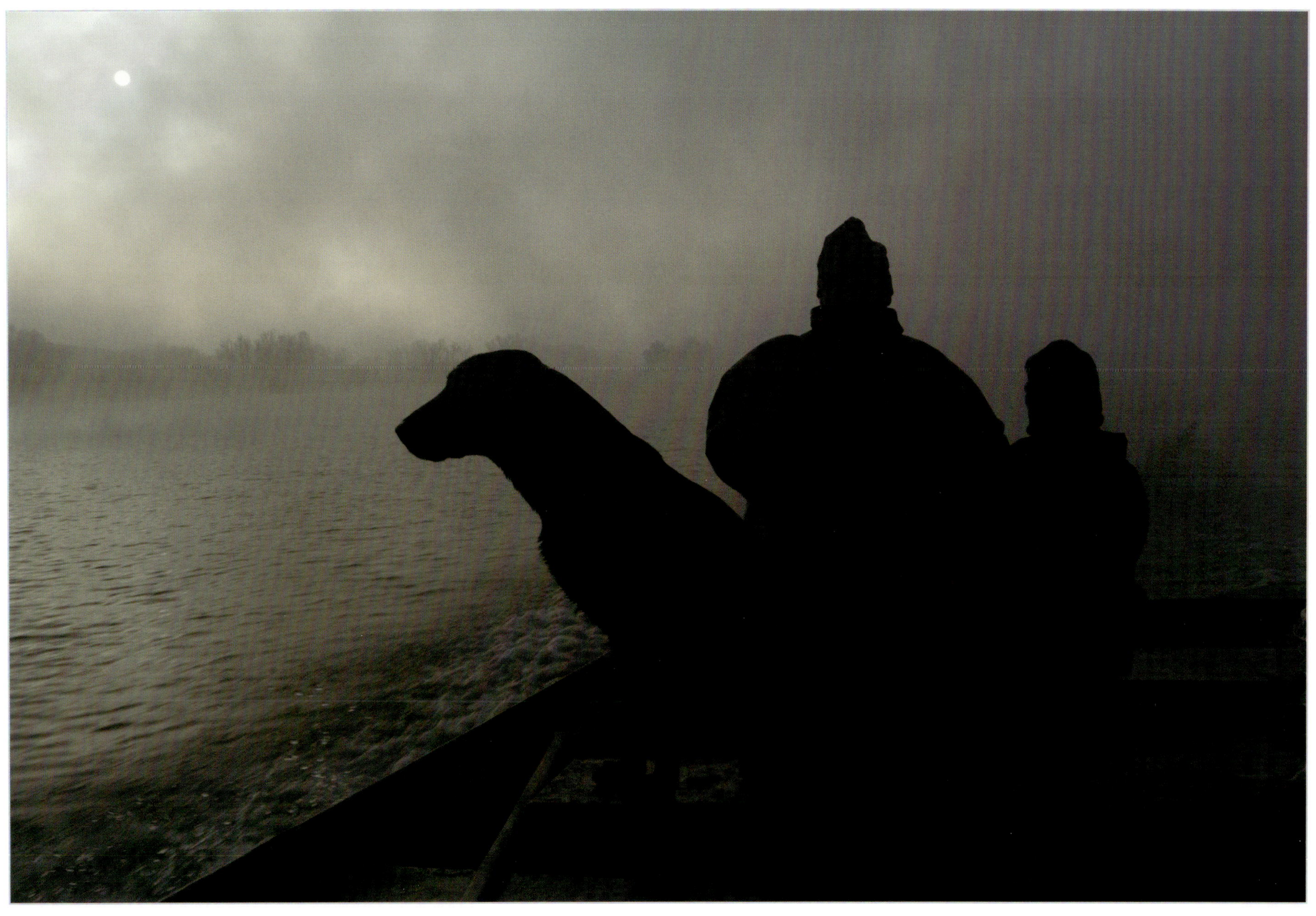

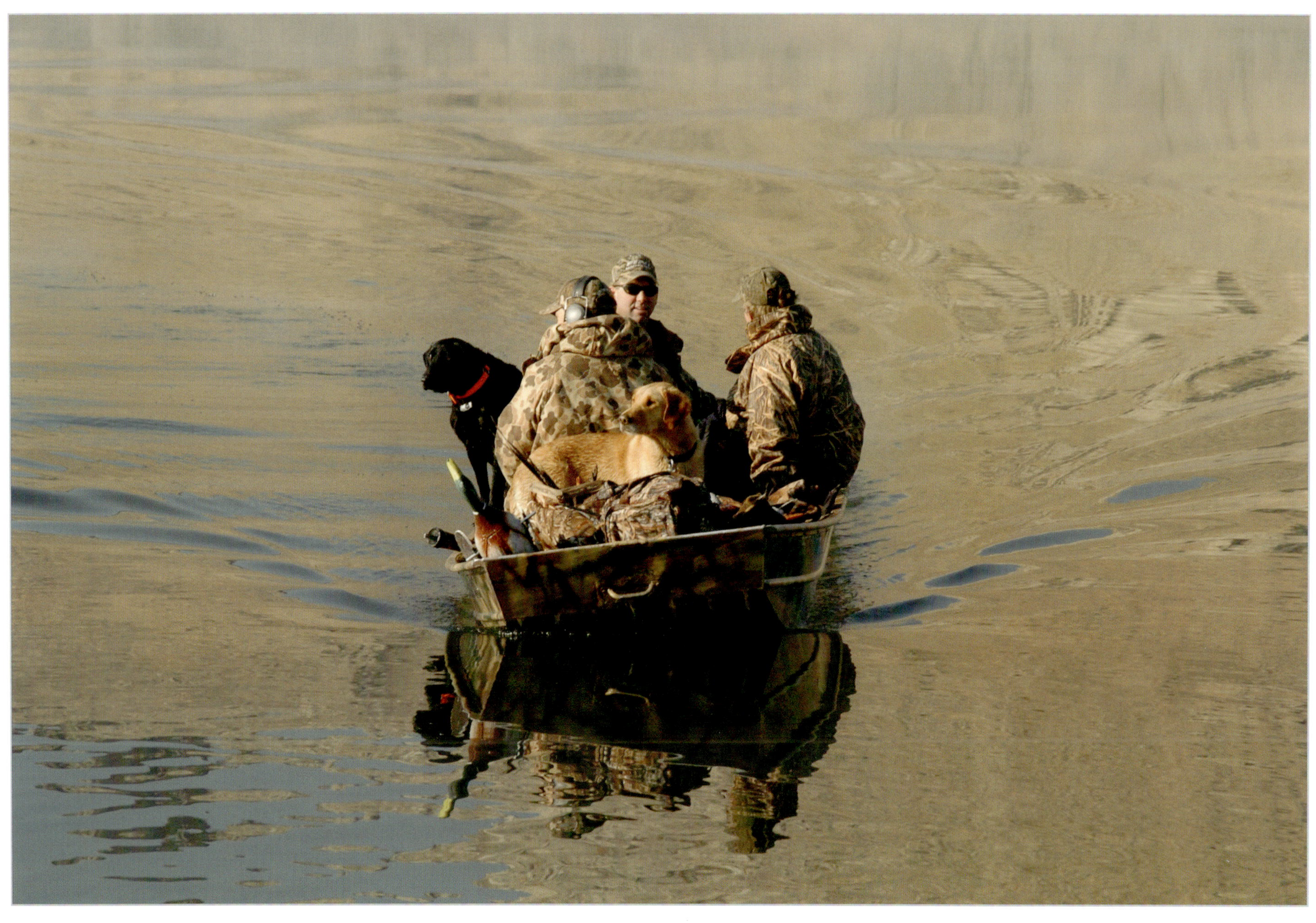

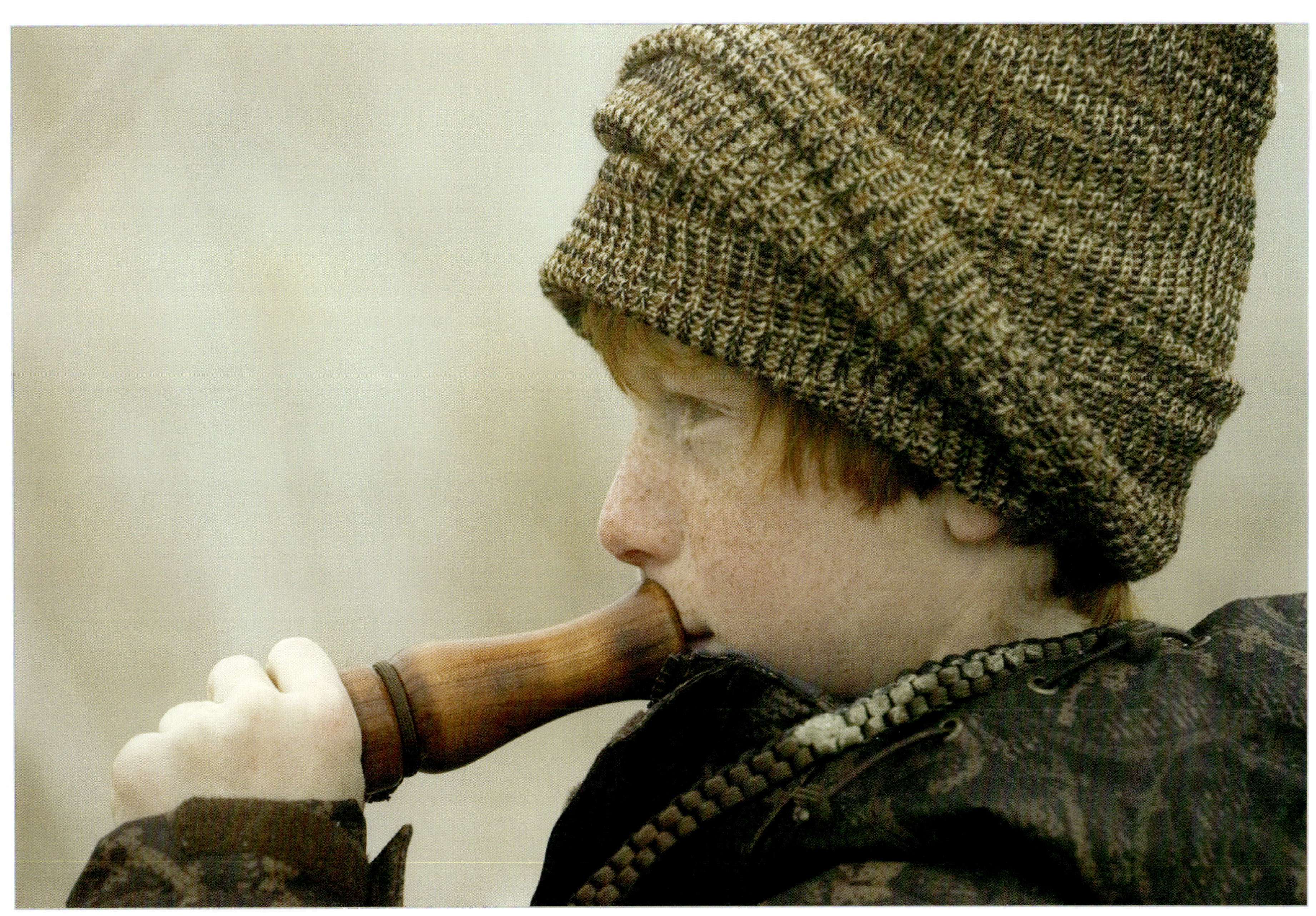

There is a passion for hunting, something deeply implanted in the human breast. ~Charles Dickens

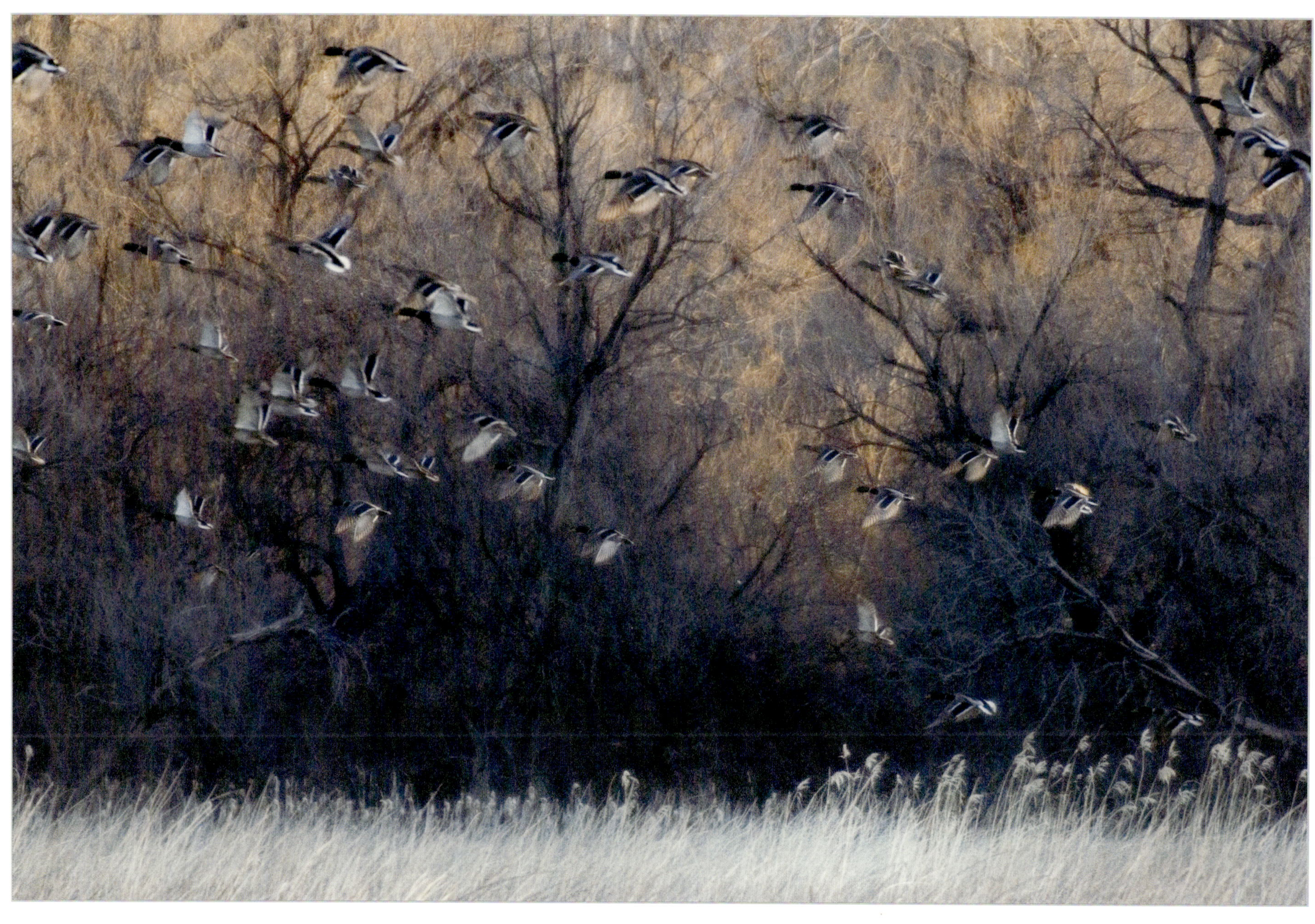

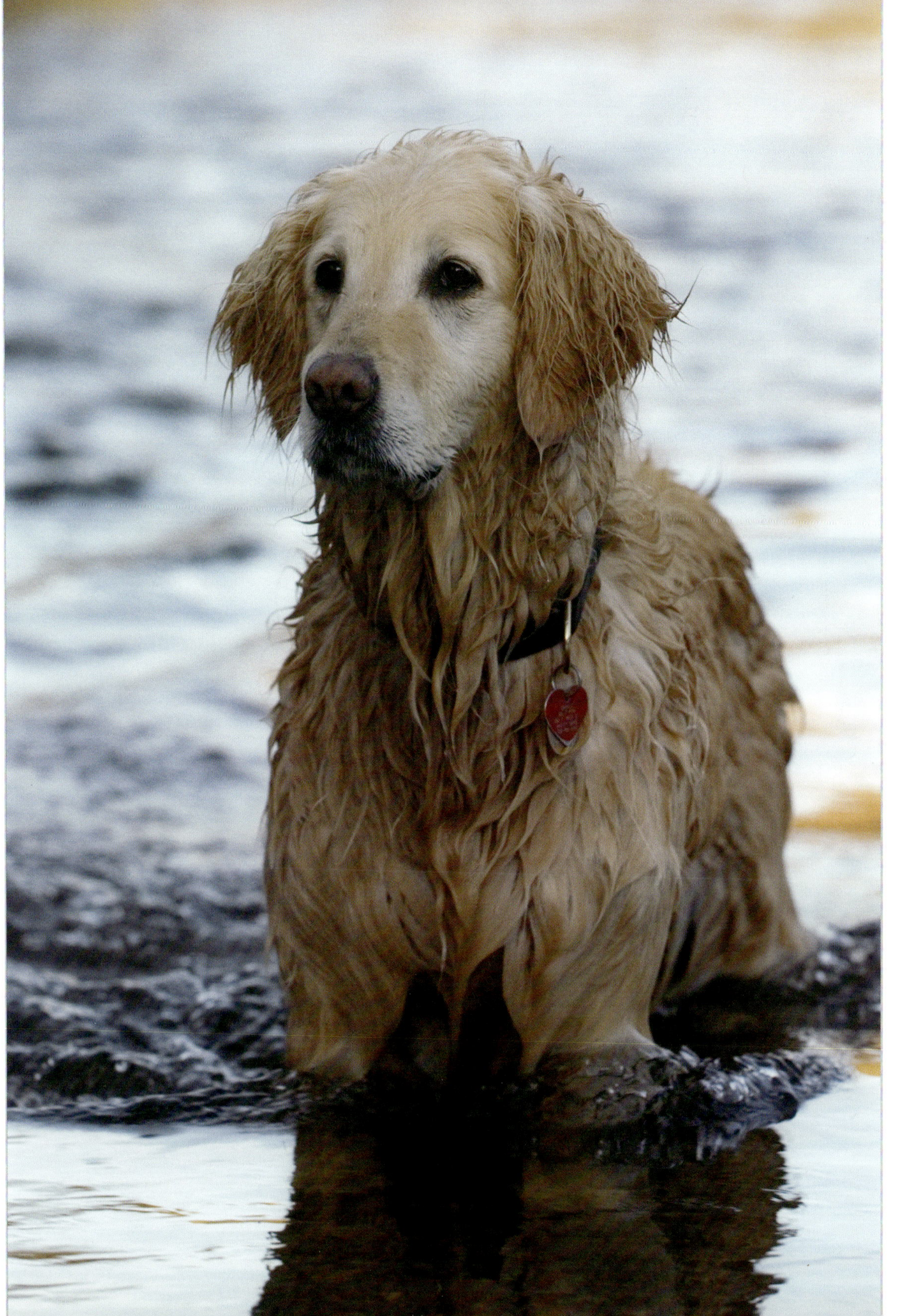

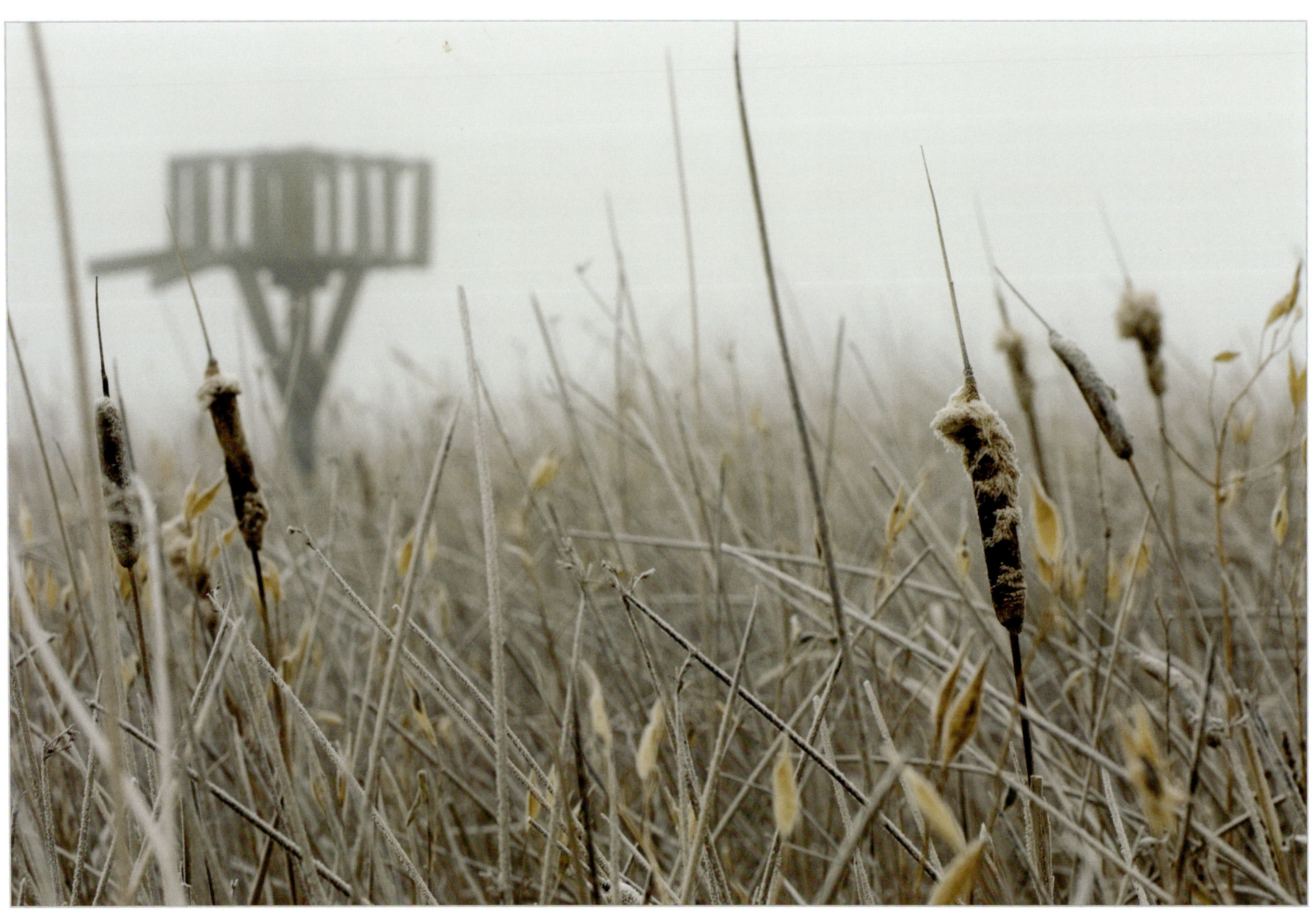

Wilderness is not a luxury but a necessity of the human spirit. ~Edward Abbey

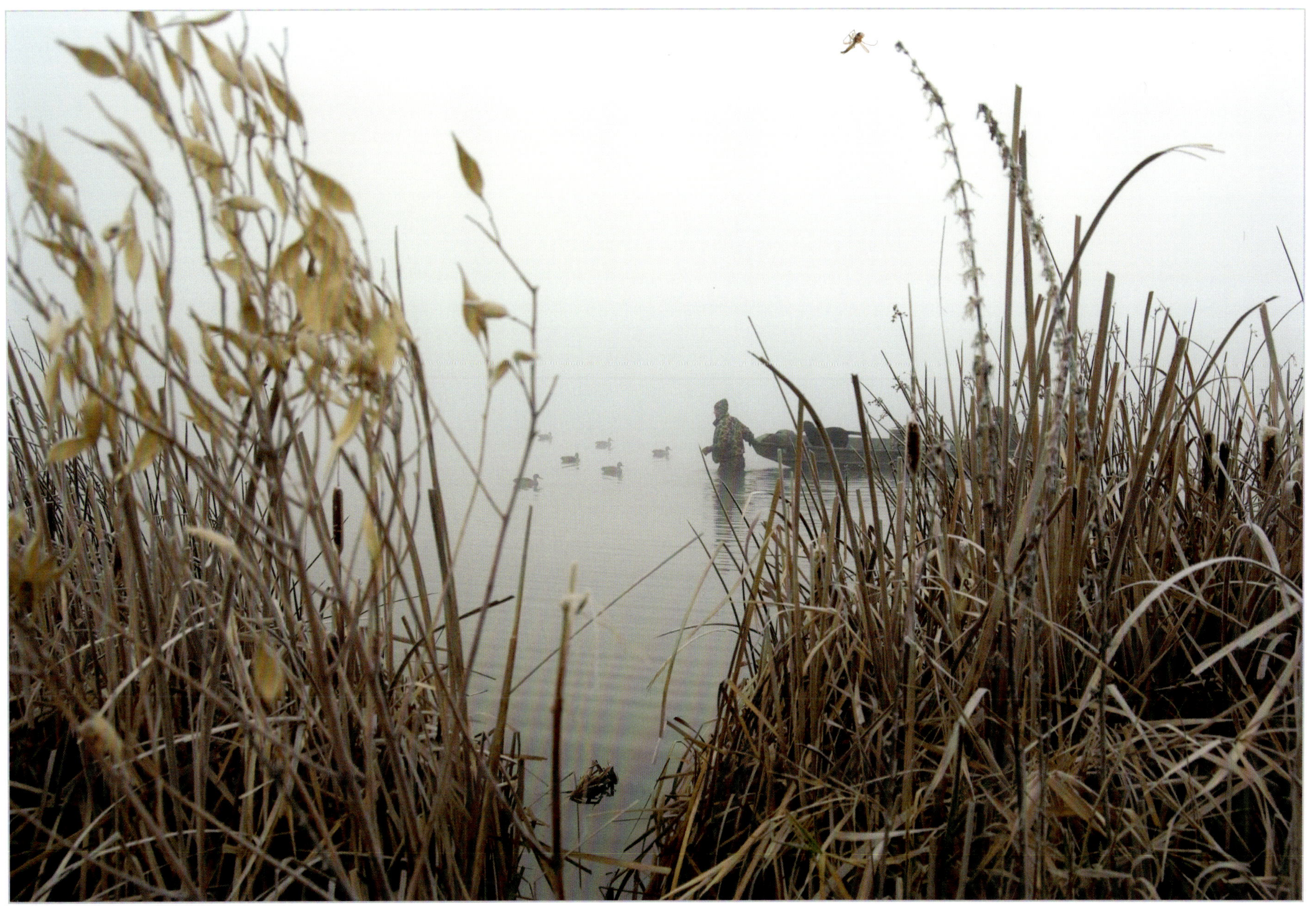

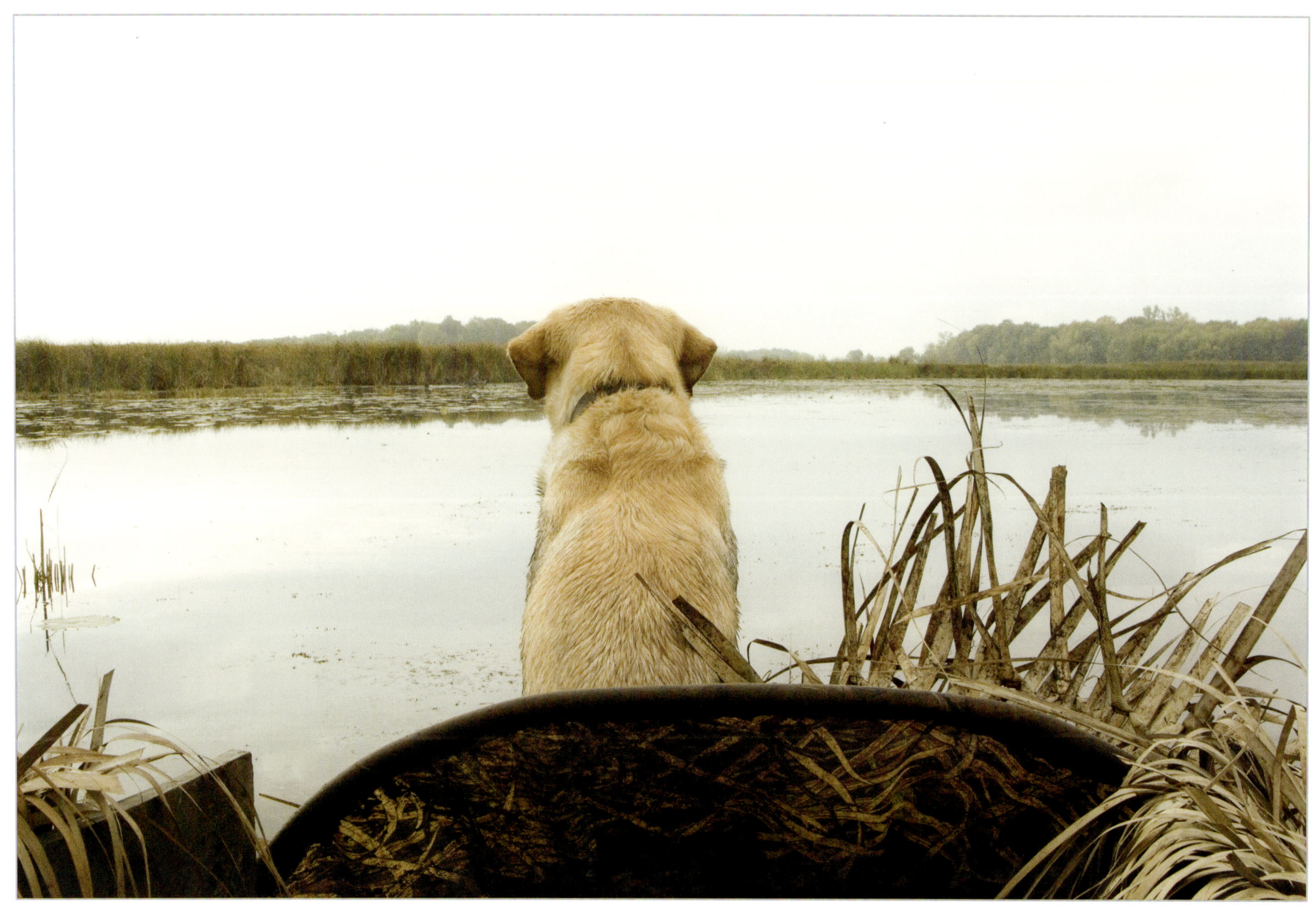

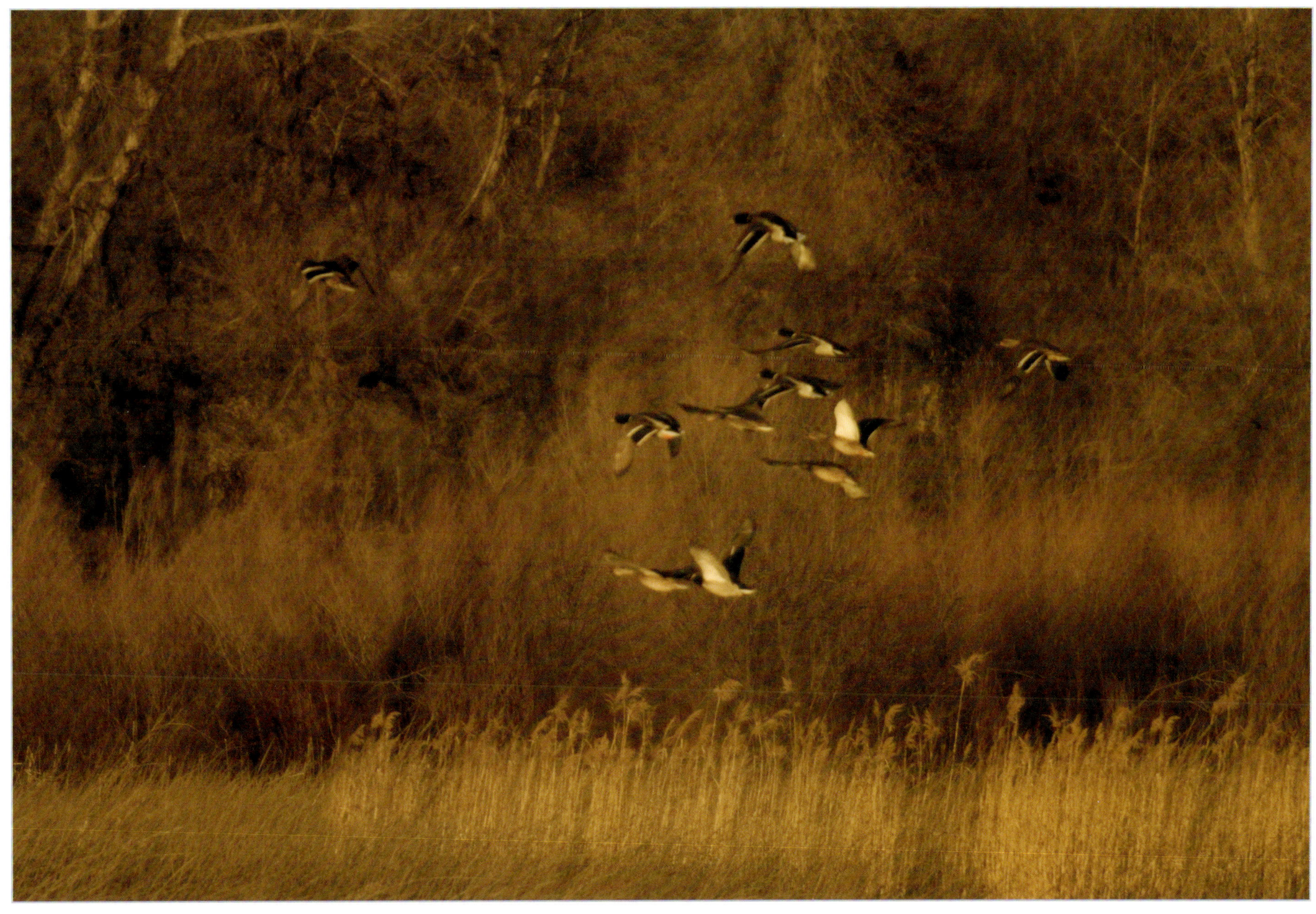

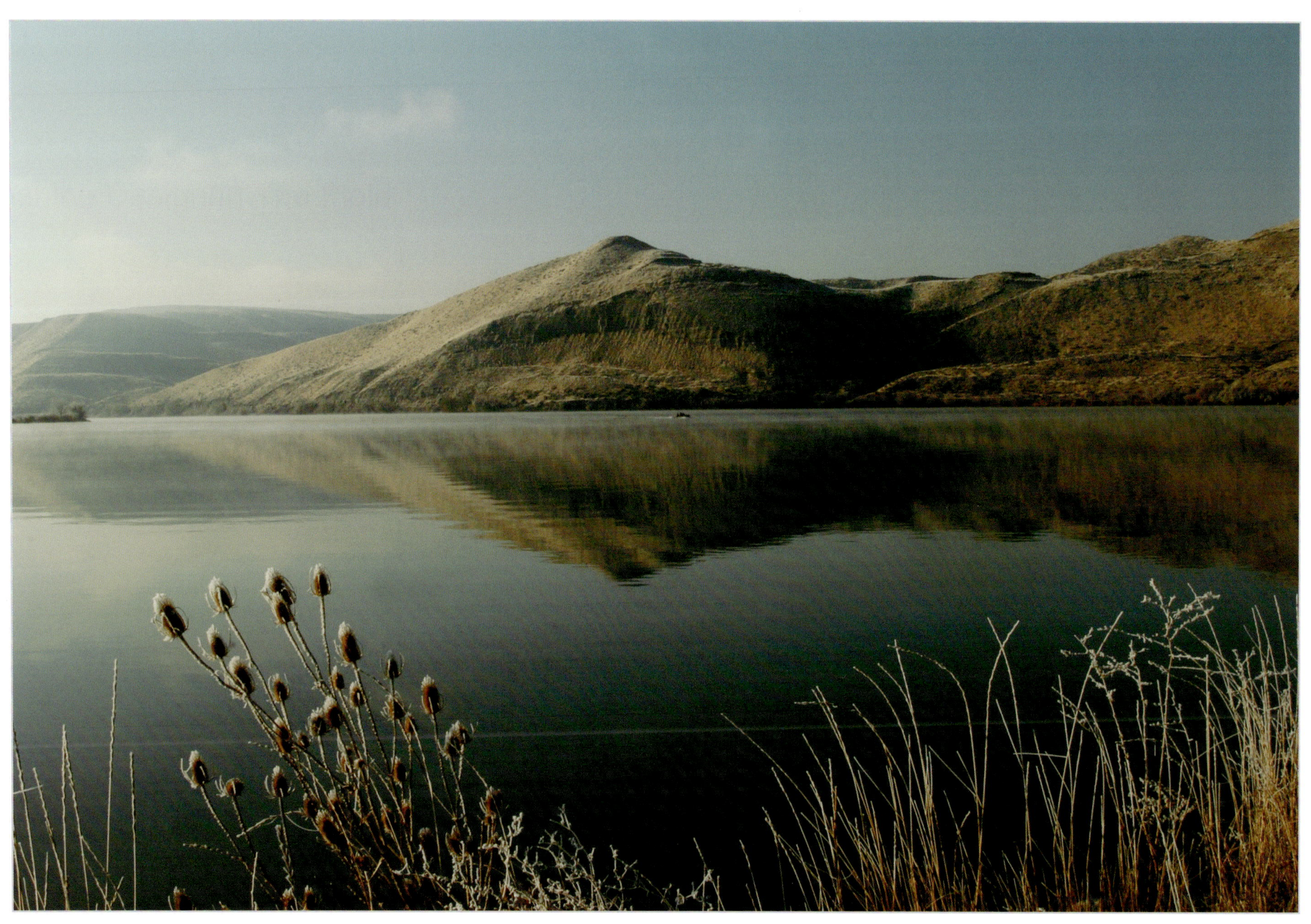

The world is but a canvas to the imagination. ~Henry David Thoreau

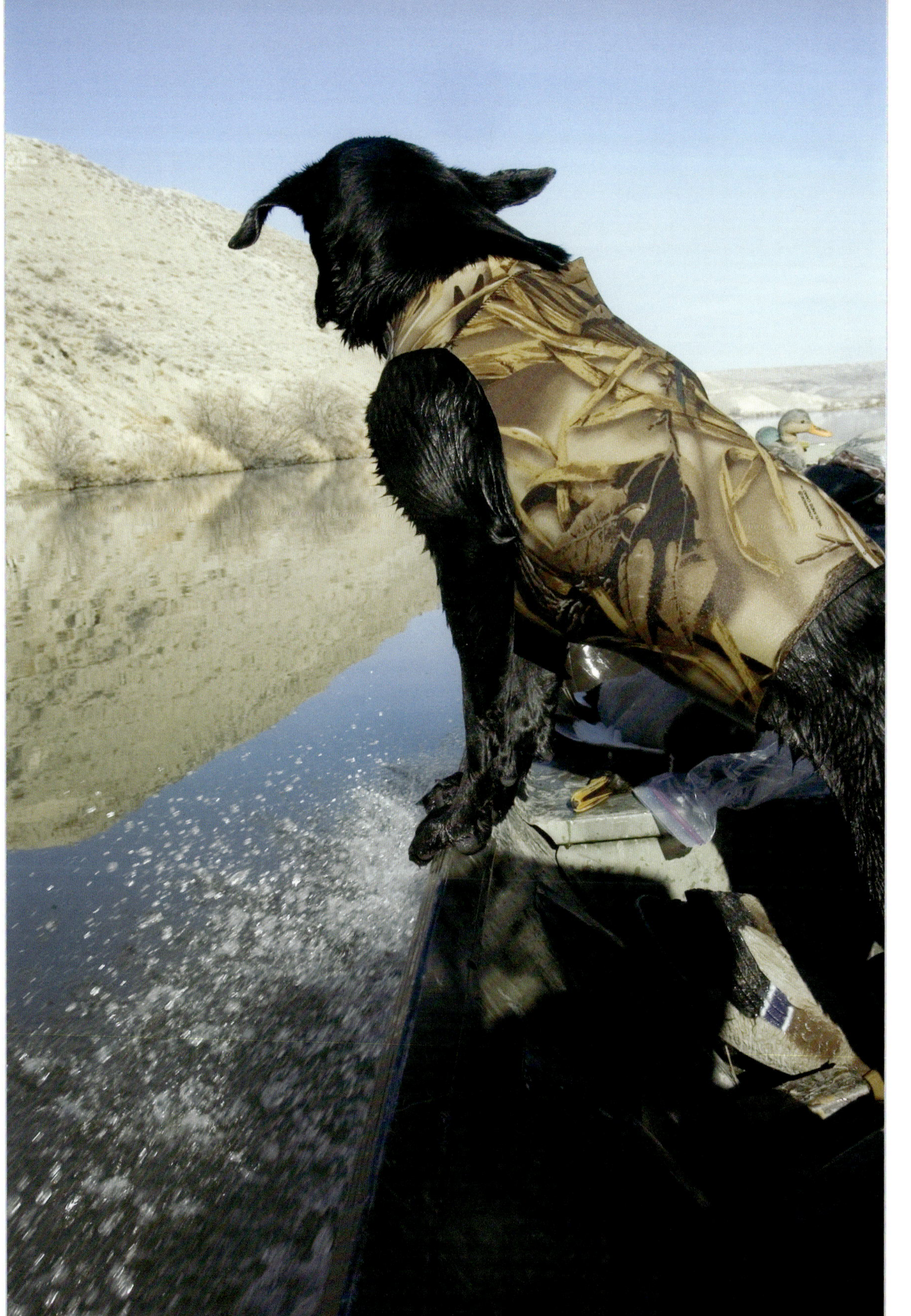

Dreams are the touchstones of our character.
~Henry David Thoreau

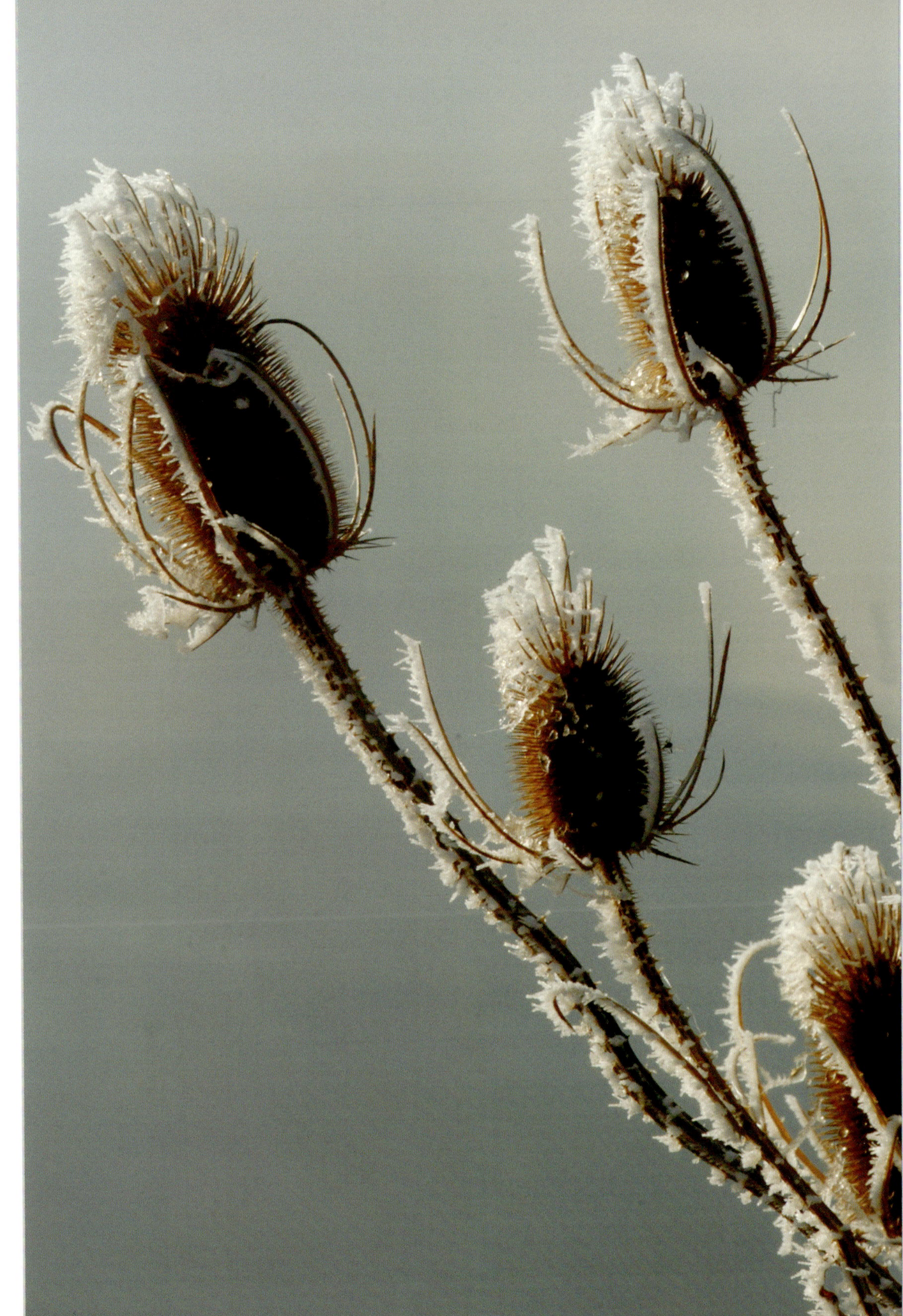

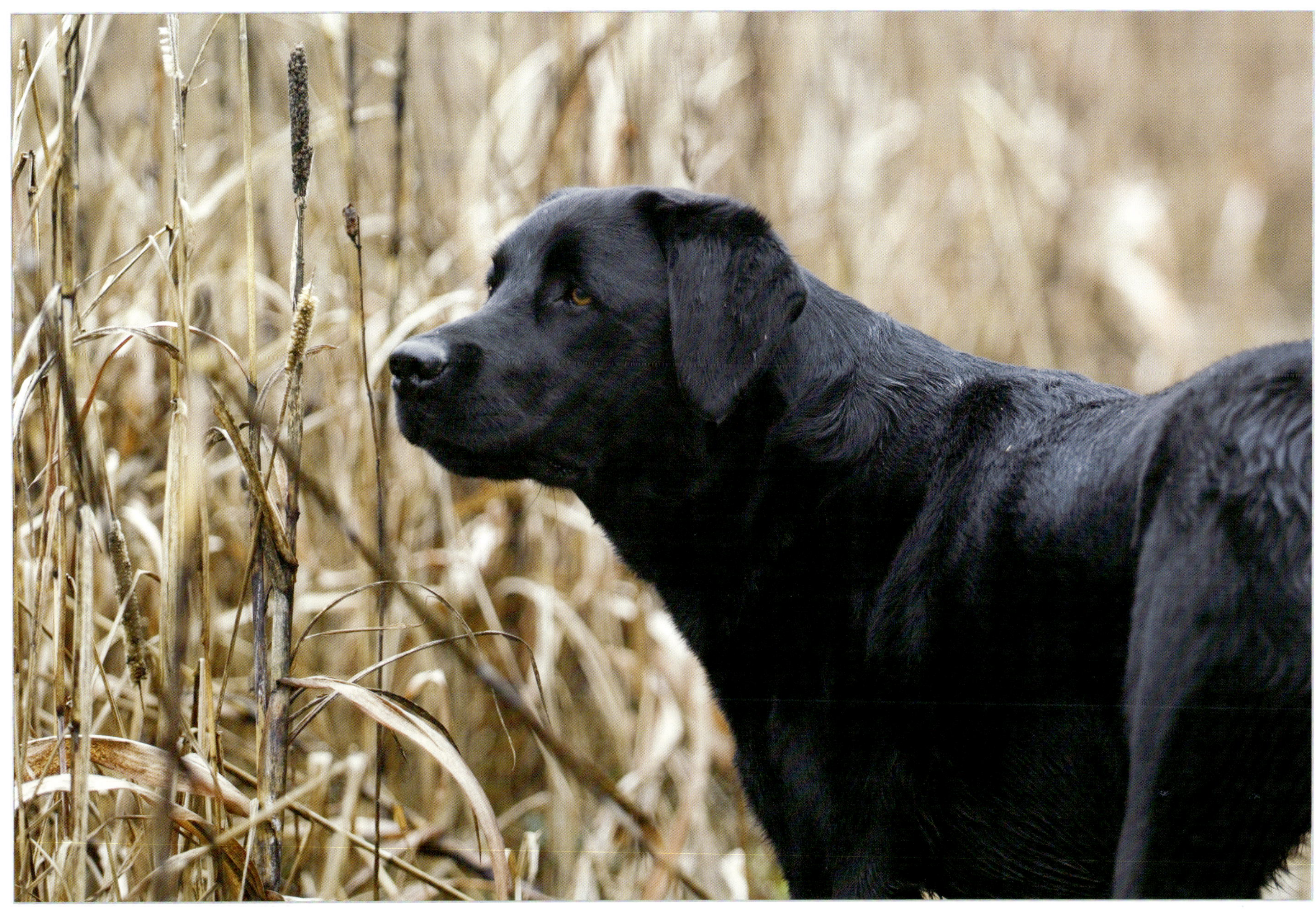

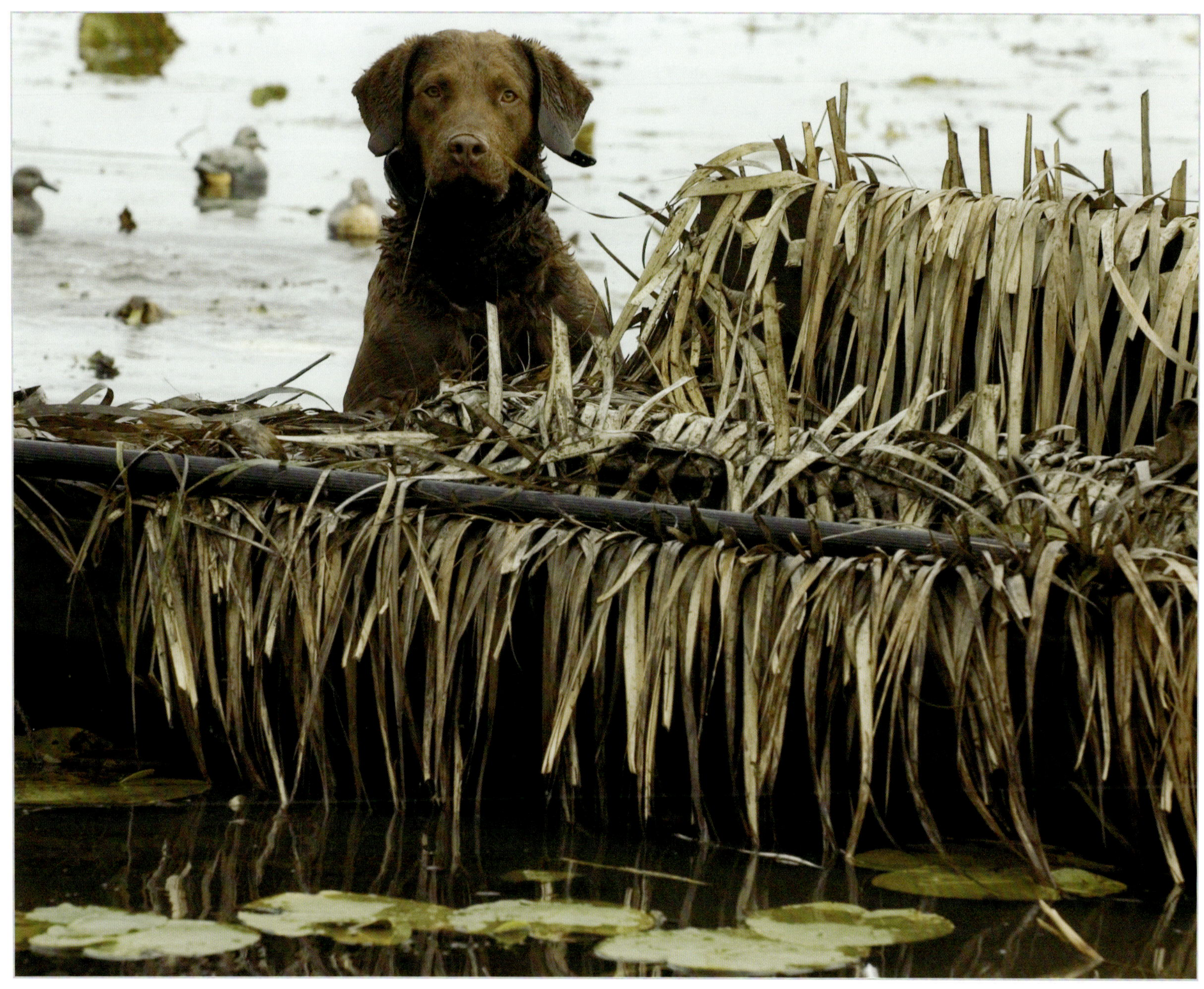

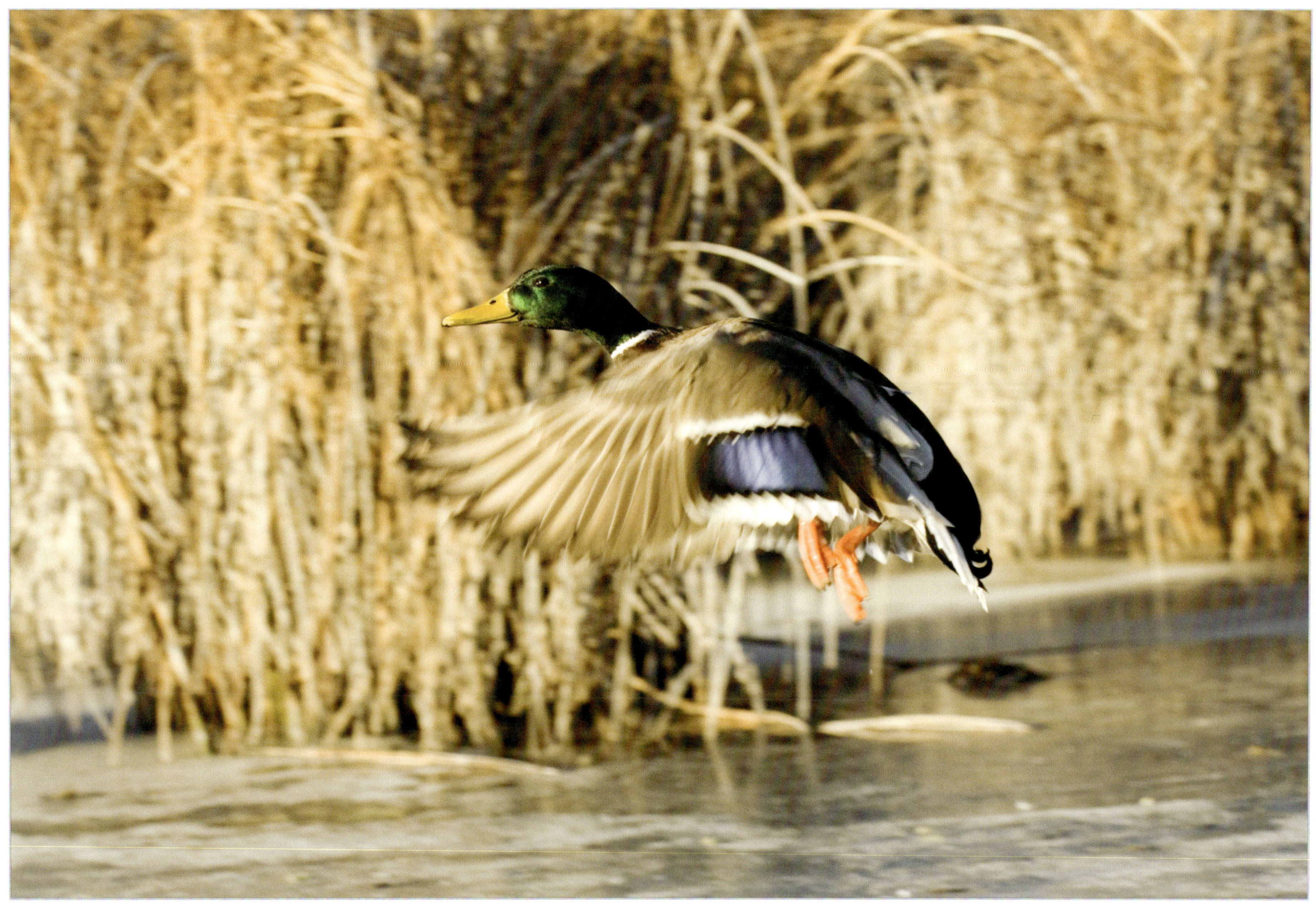

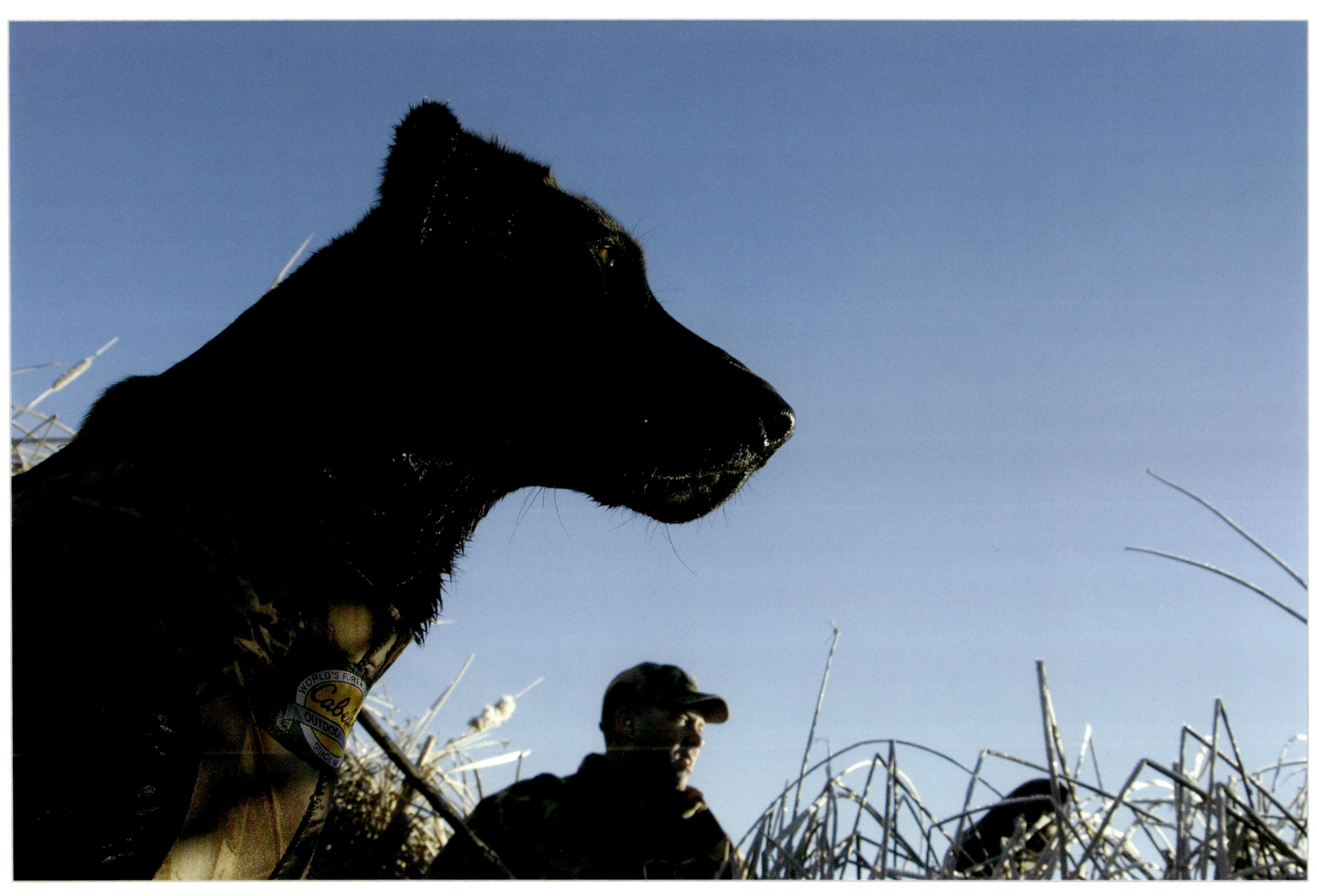

When you have shot one bird flying you have shot all birds flying. They are all different and they fly in different ways but the sensation is the same and the last one is as good as the first. ~Ernest Hemingway.

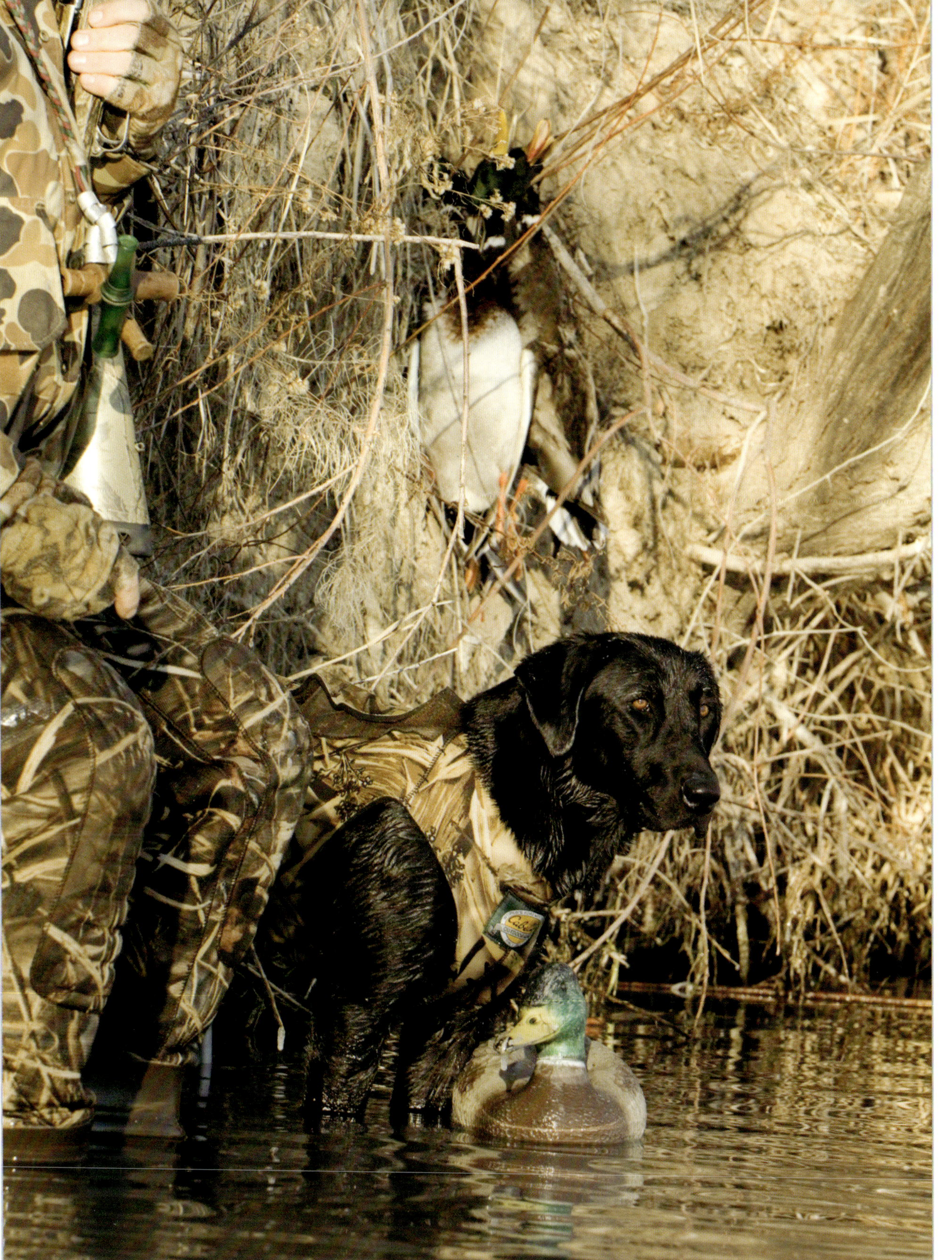

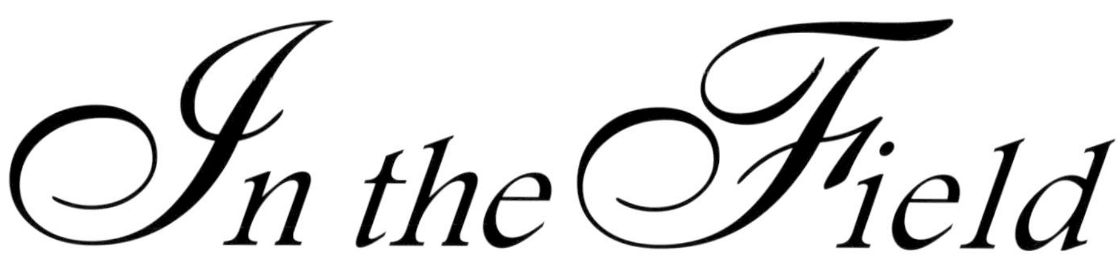

A true photograph need not be explained,
nor can it be contained in words. ~Ansel Adams

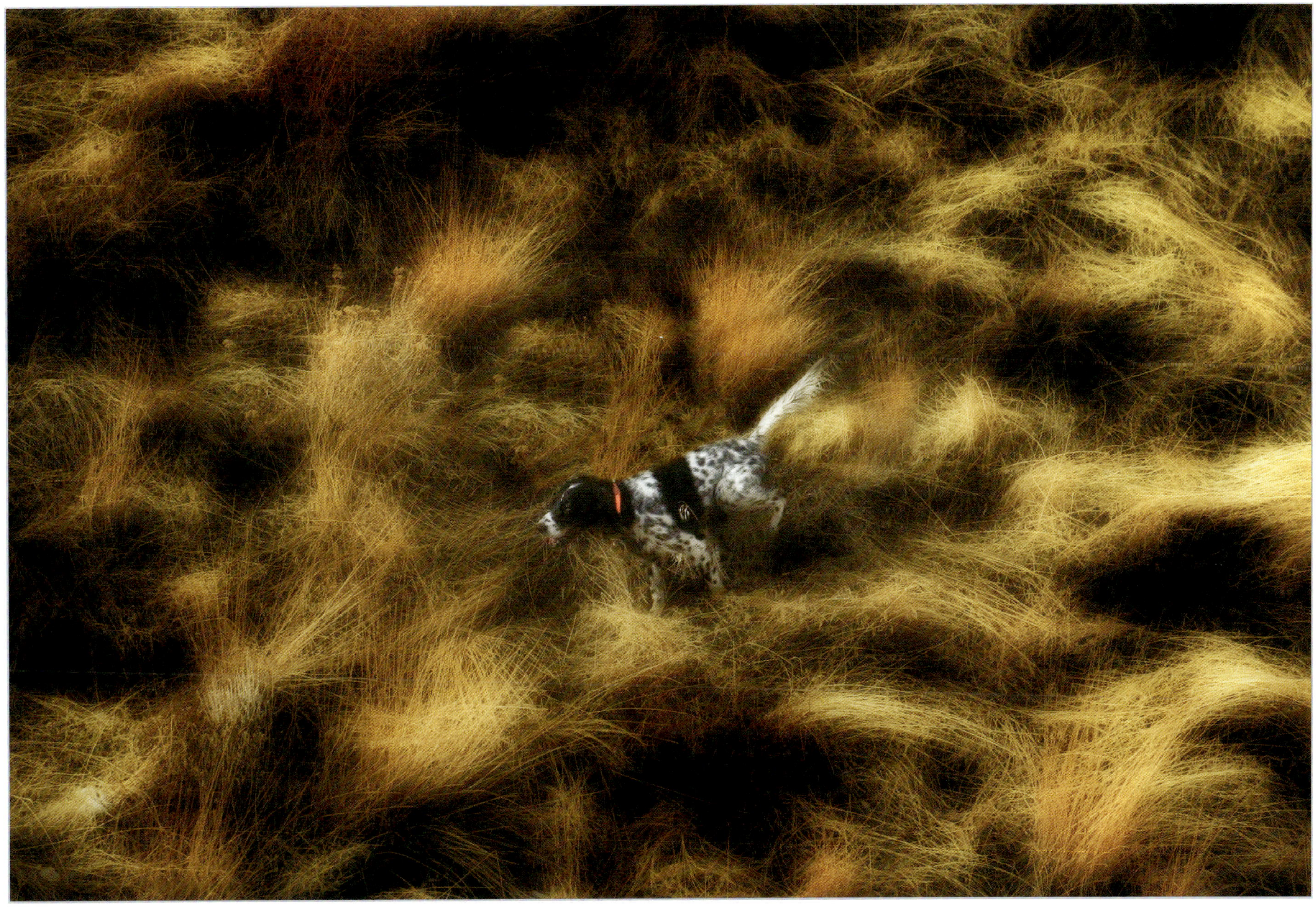

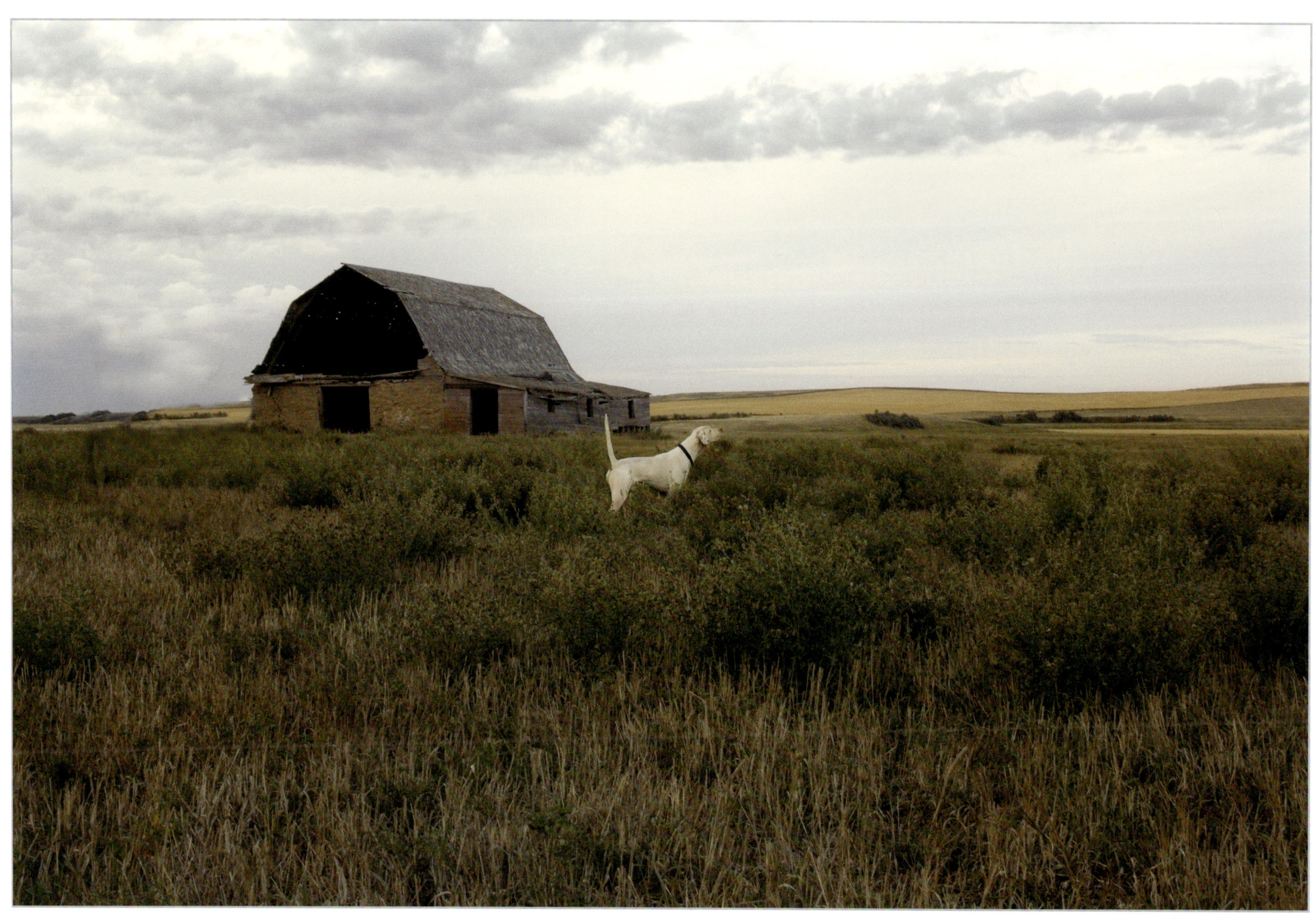

The real voyage of discovery consists not in seeking new landscapes, but in having new eyes. ~*Marcel Proust*

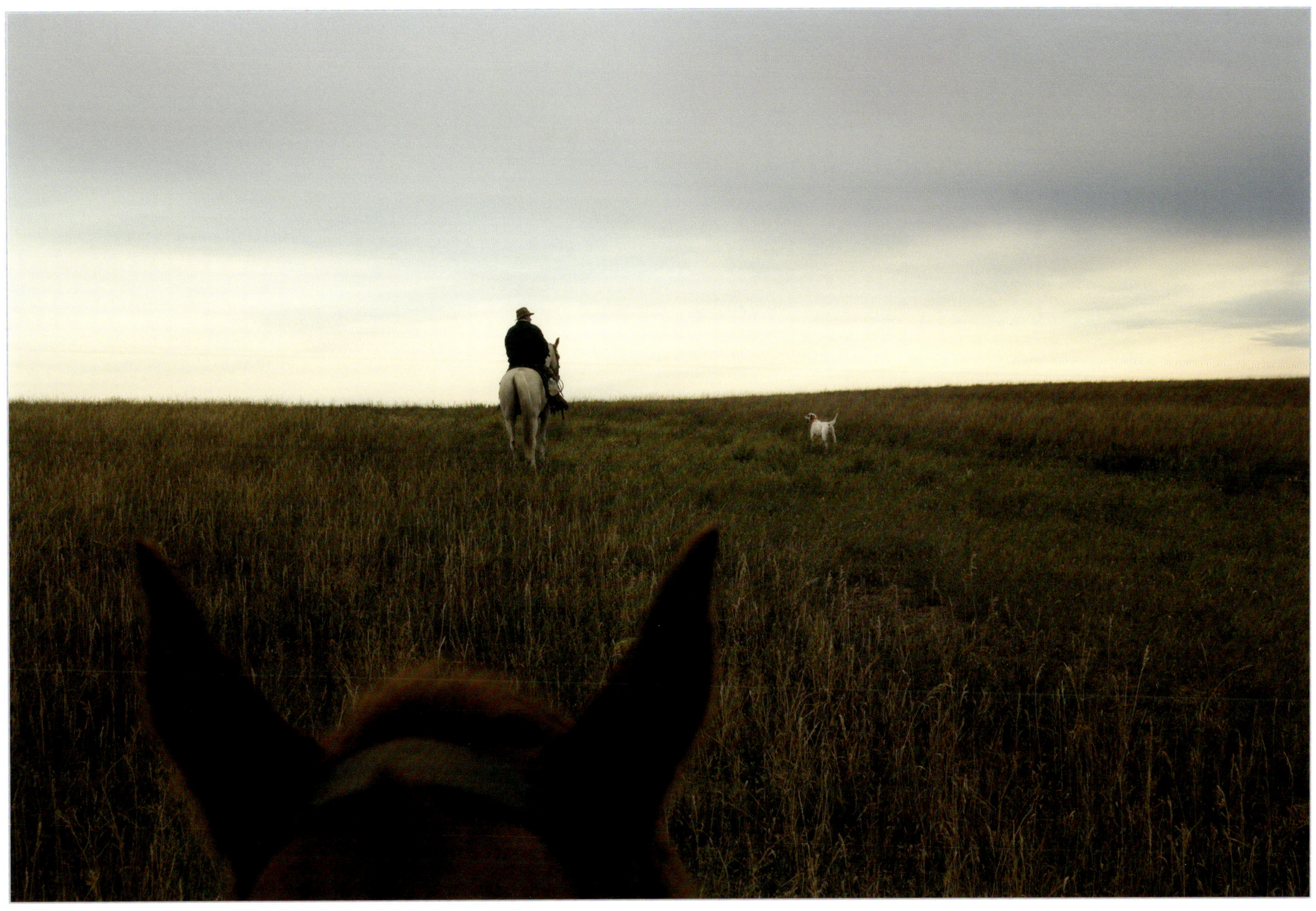

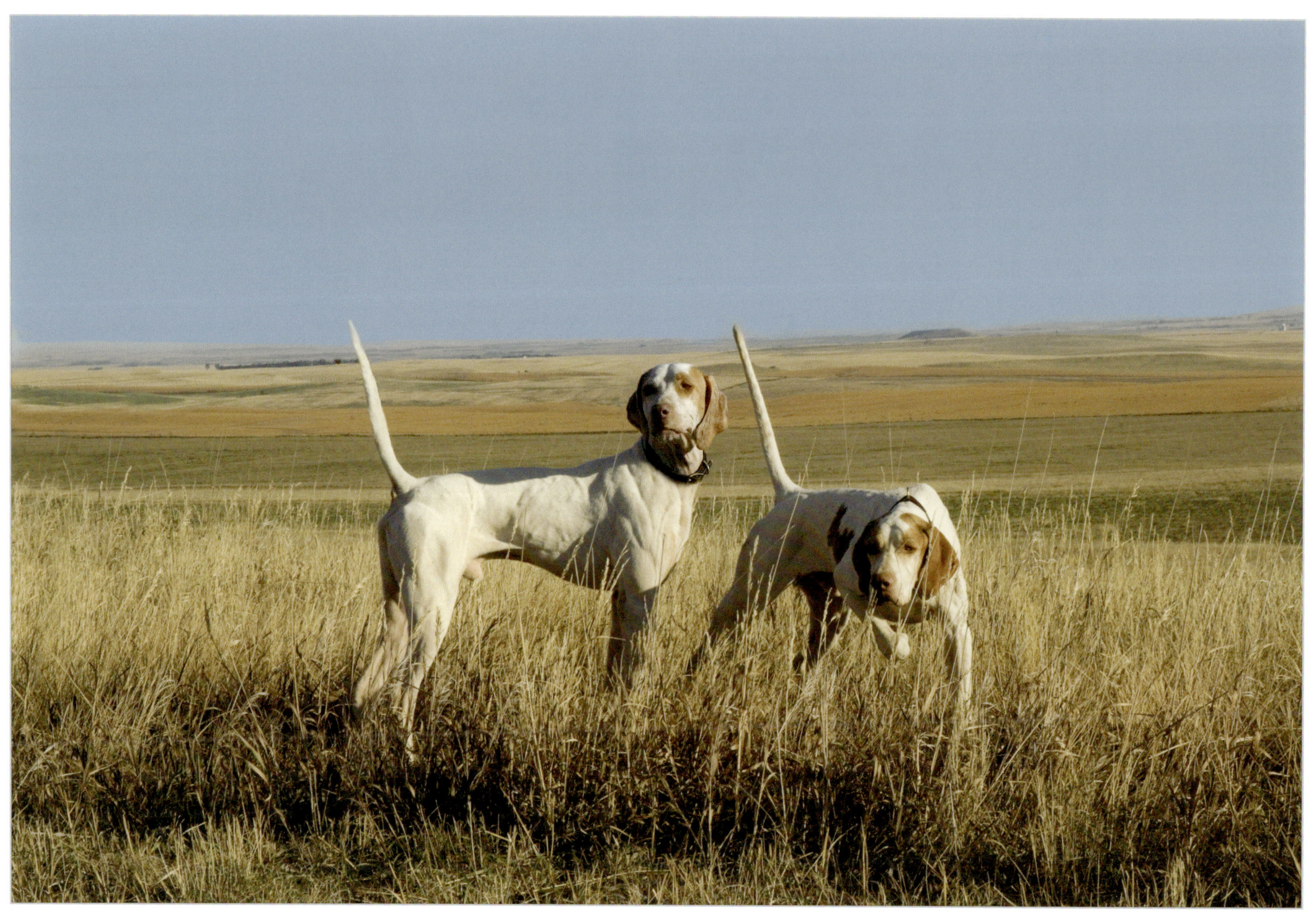

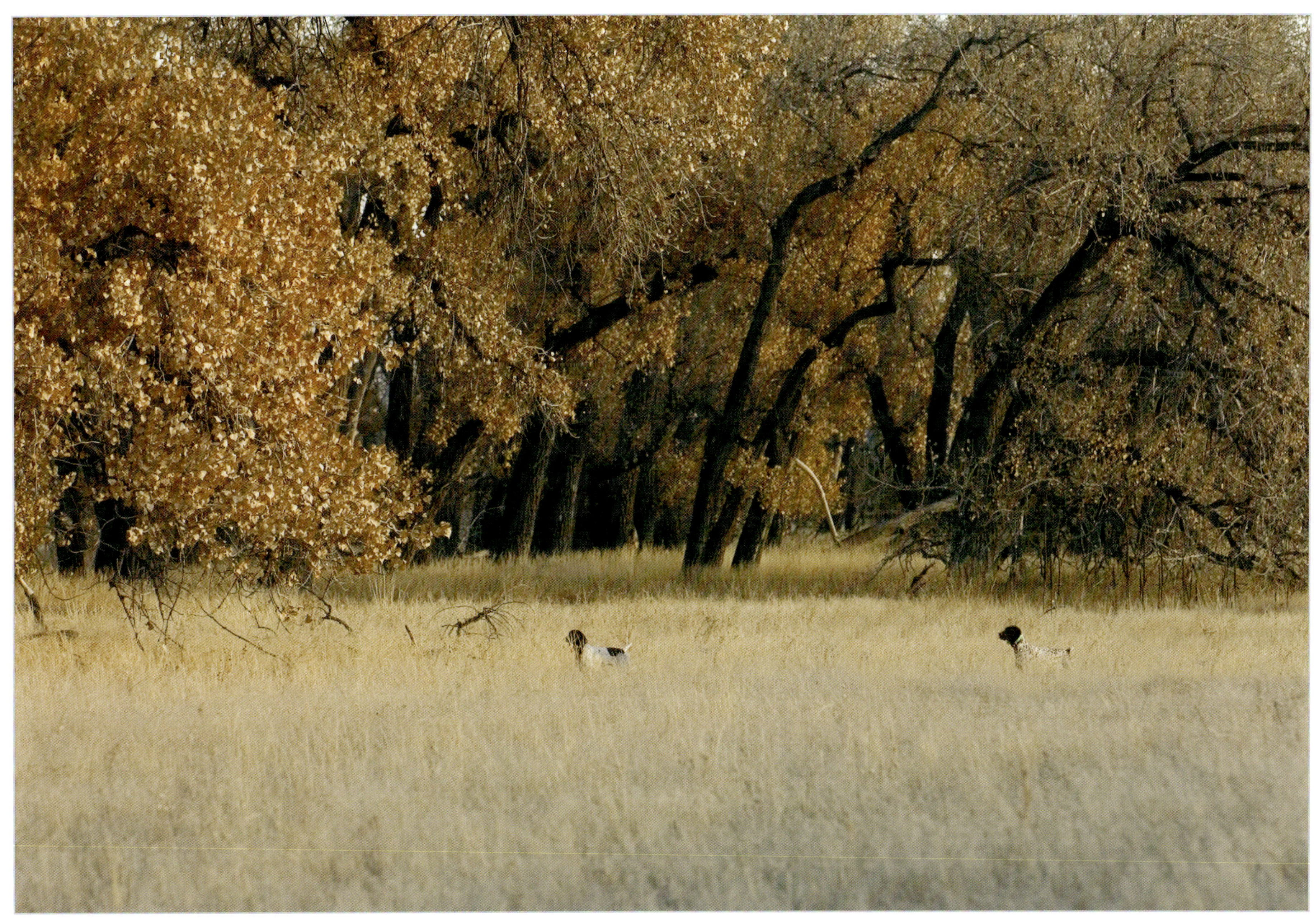

The richness I achieve comes from Nature, the source of my inspiration. ~Claude Monet

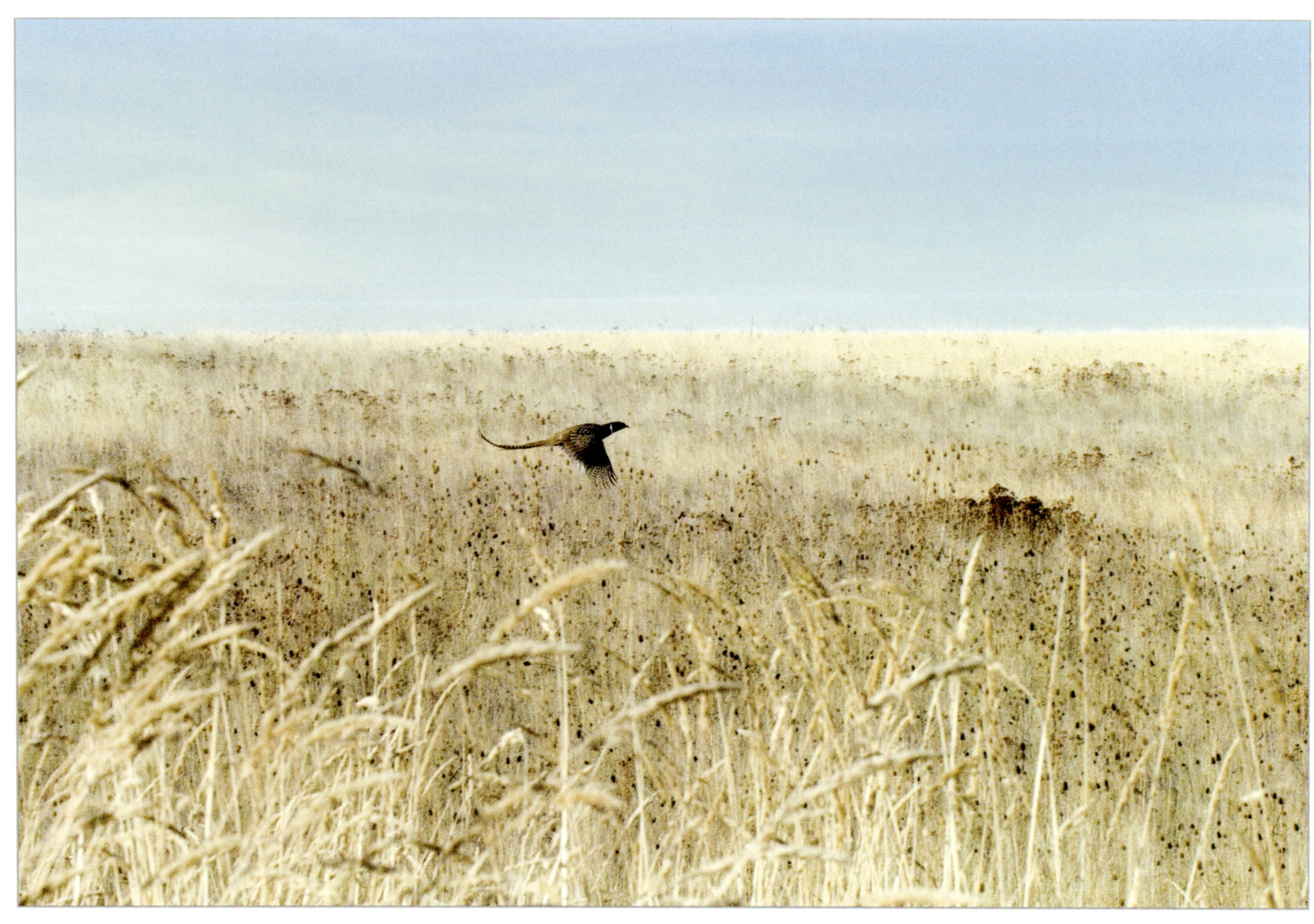

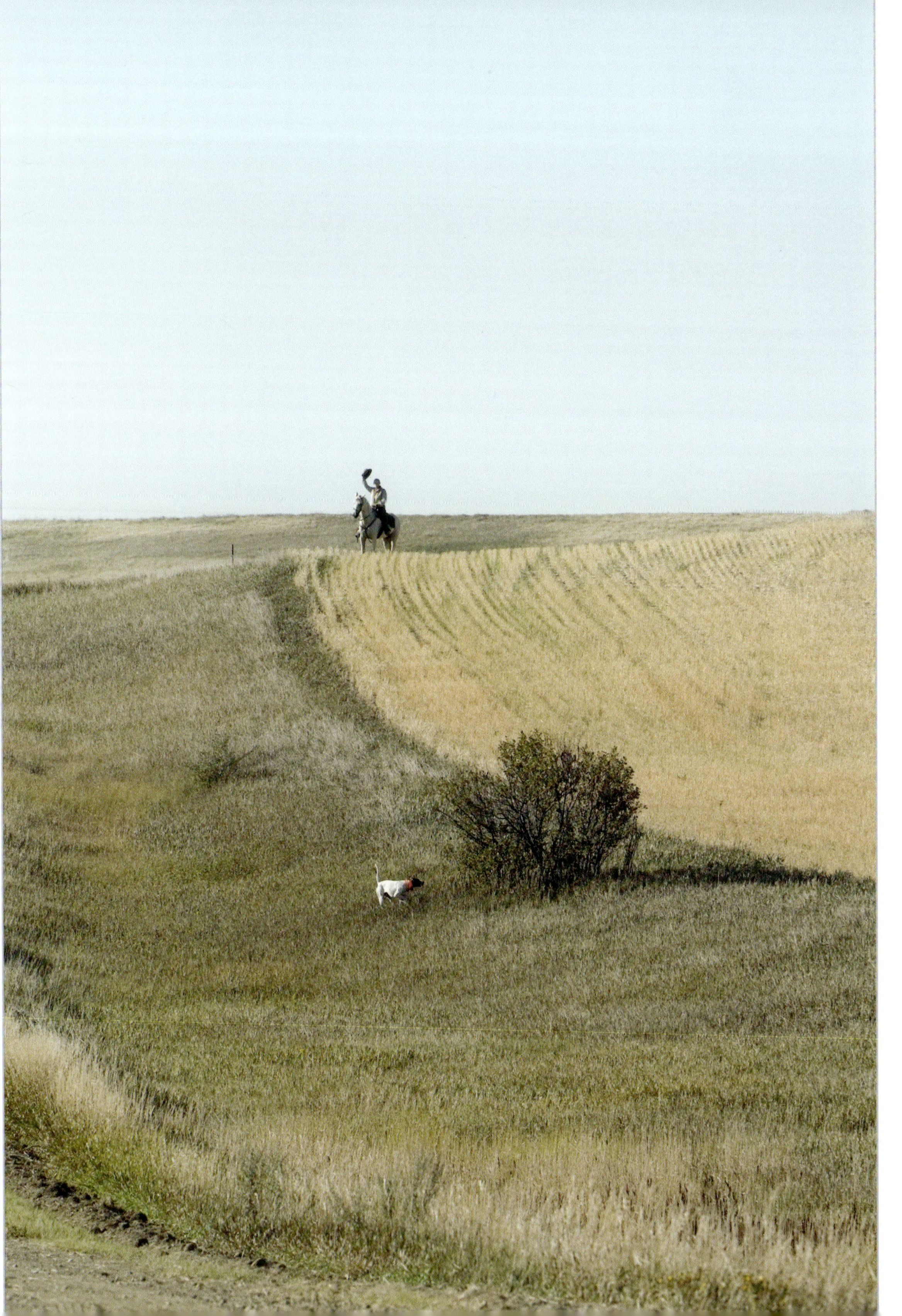

When words become unclear, I shall focus with photographs. When images become inadequate, I shall be content with silence.
~Ansel Adams

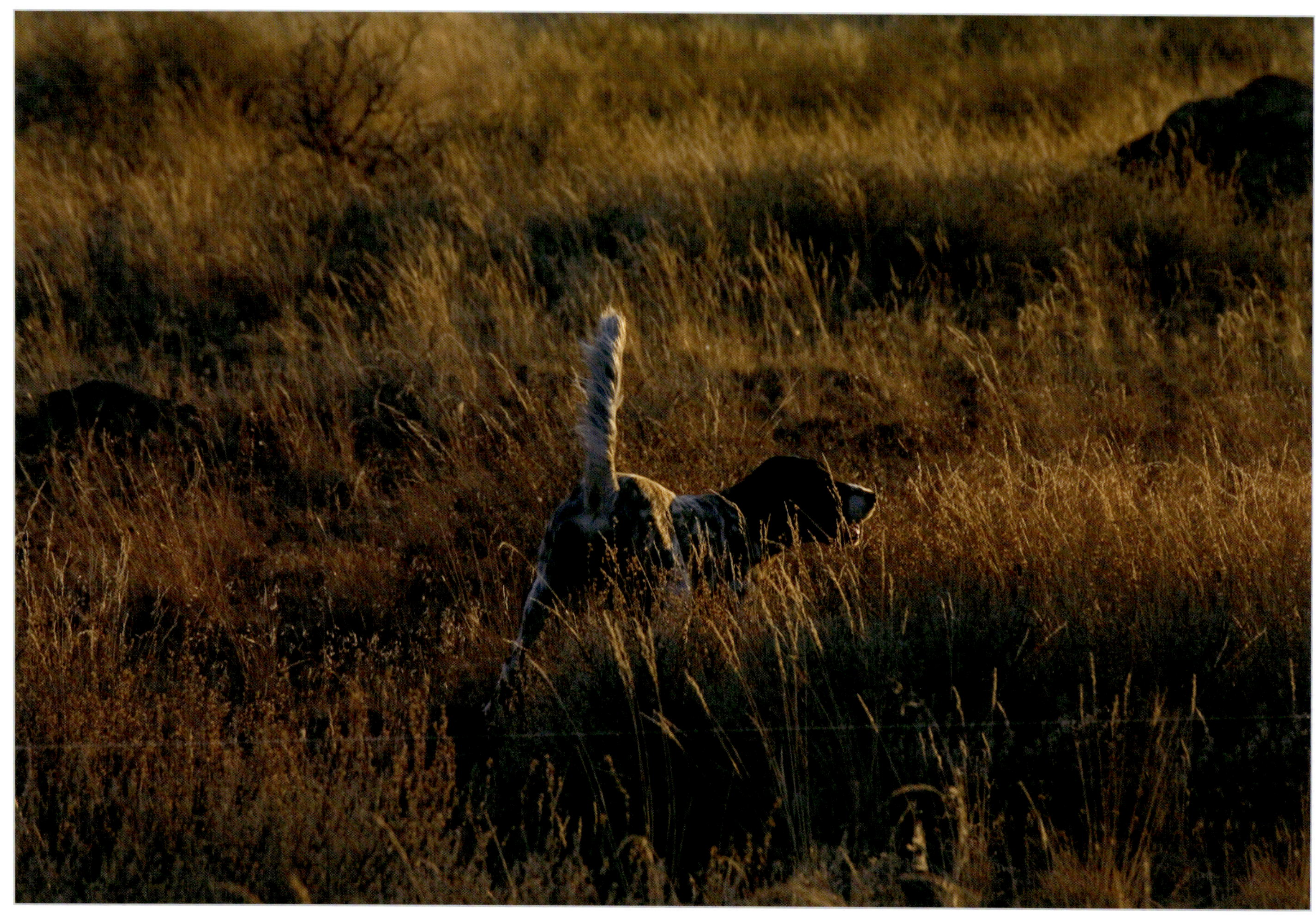

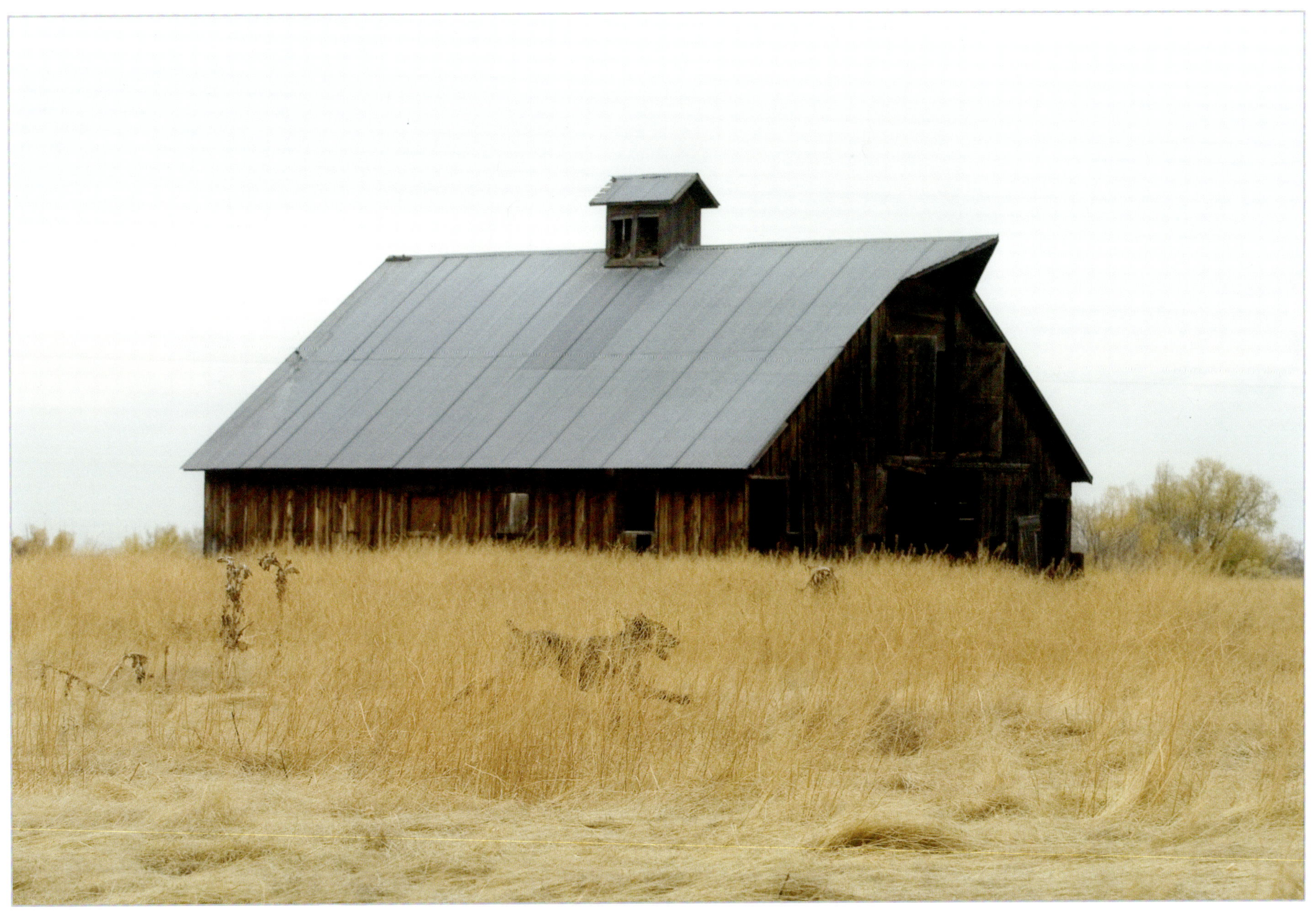

In wisdom gathered over time
I have found that every experience
is a form of exploration.
~Ansel Adams

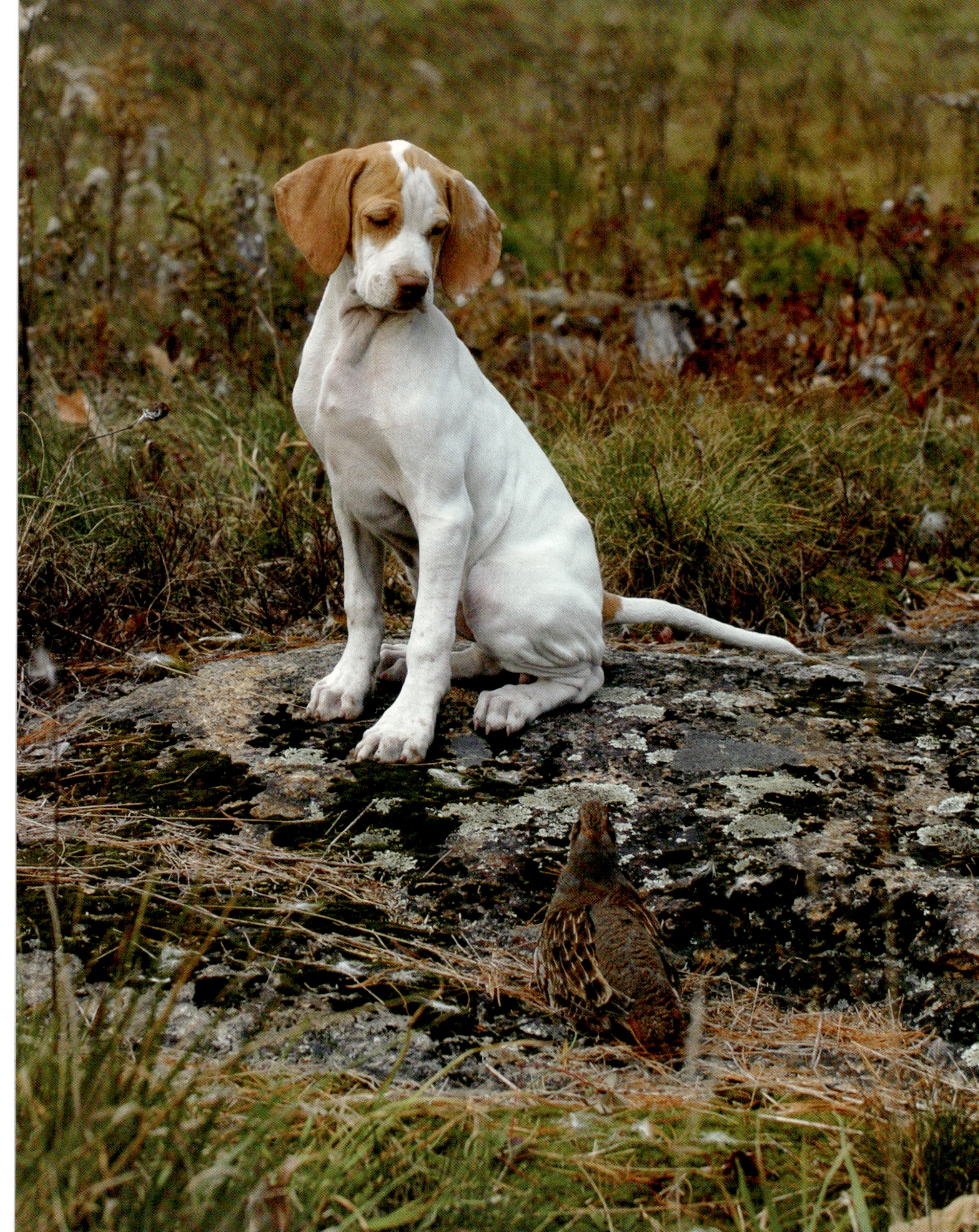

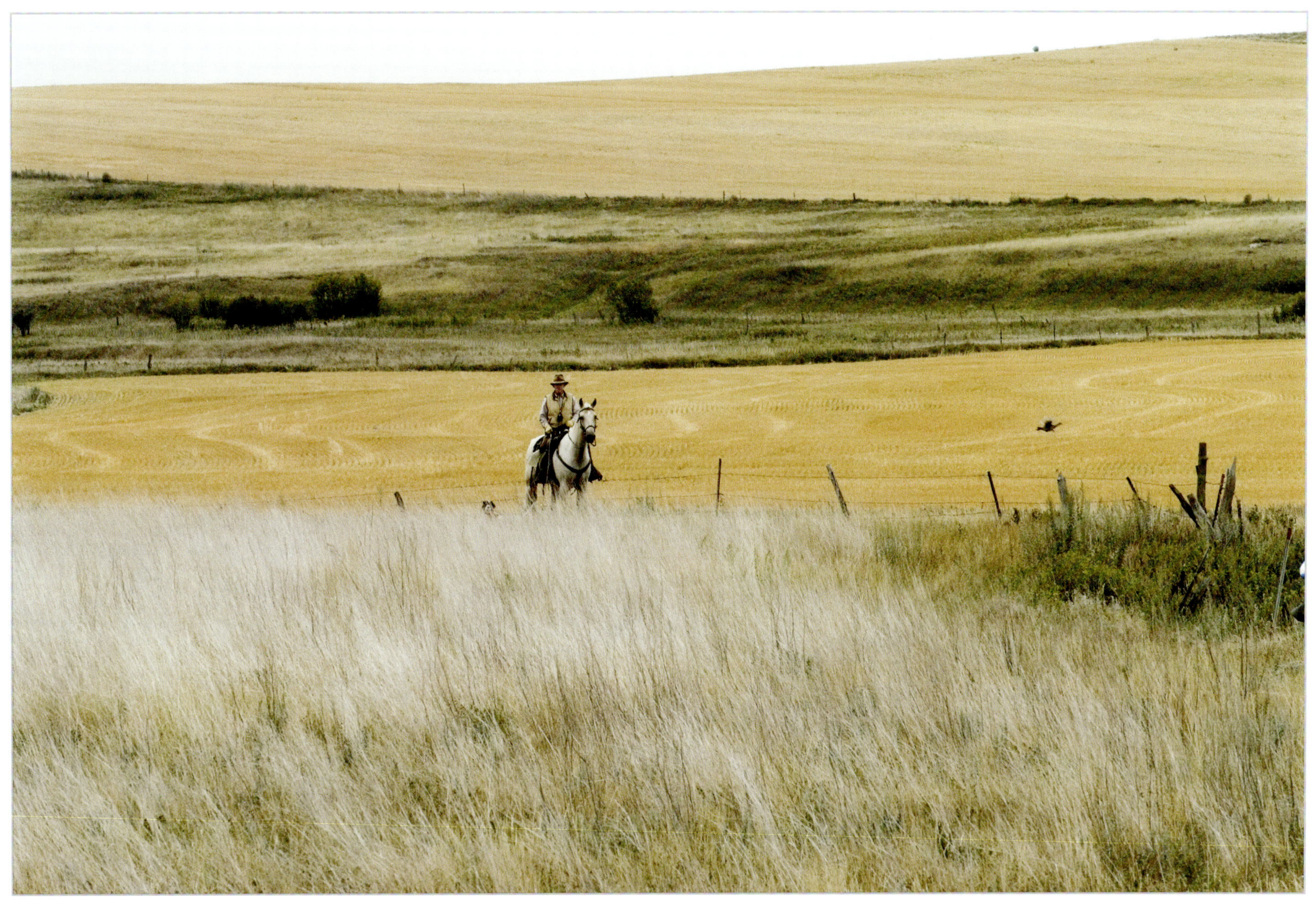

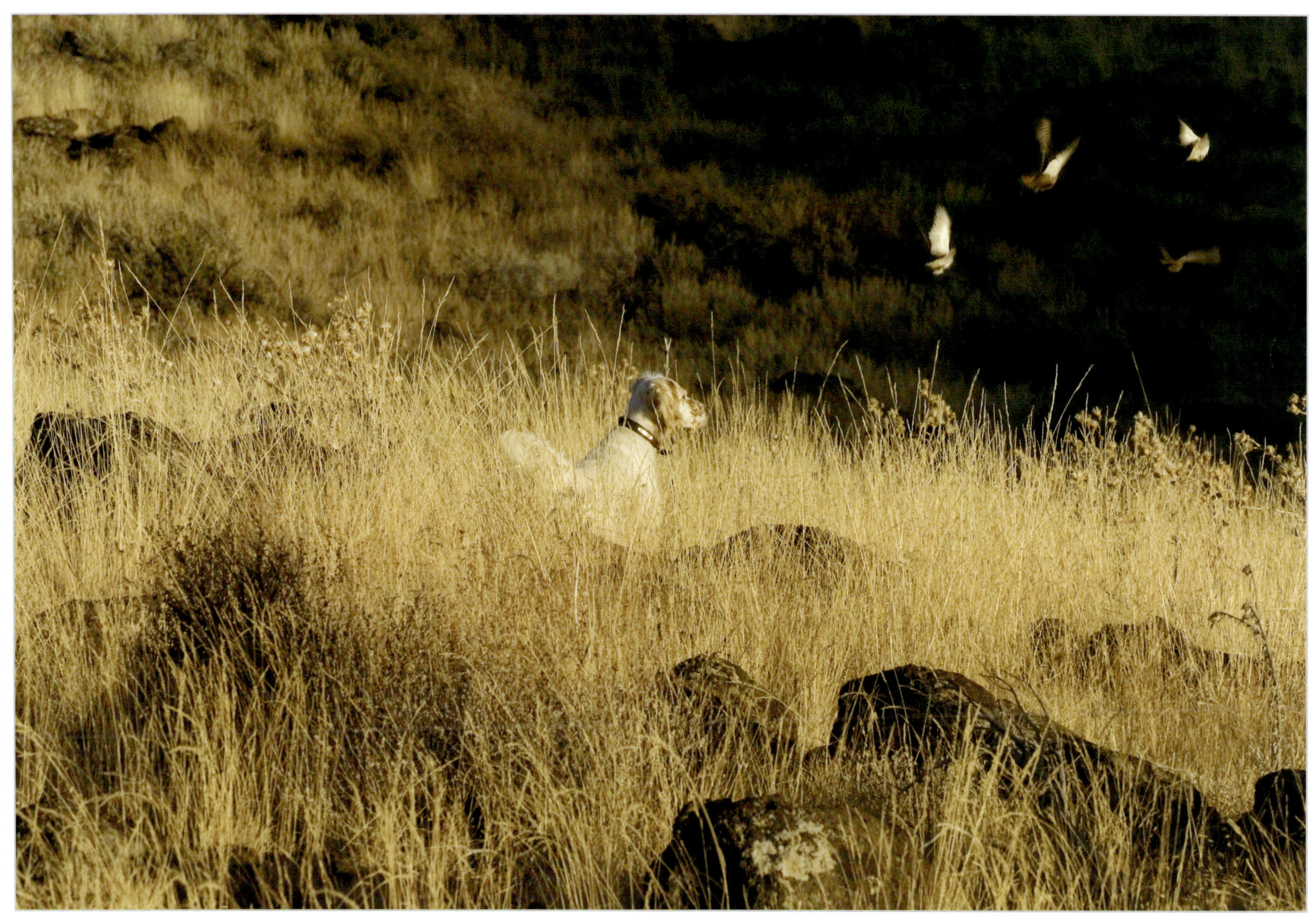

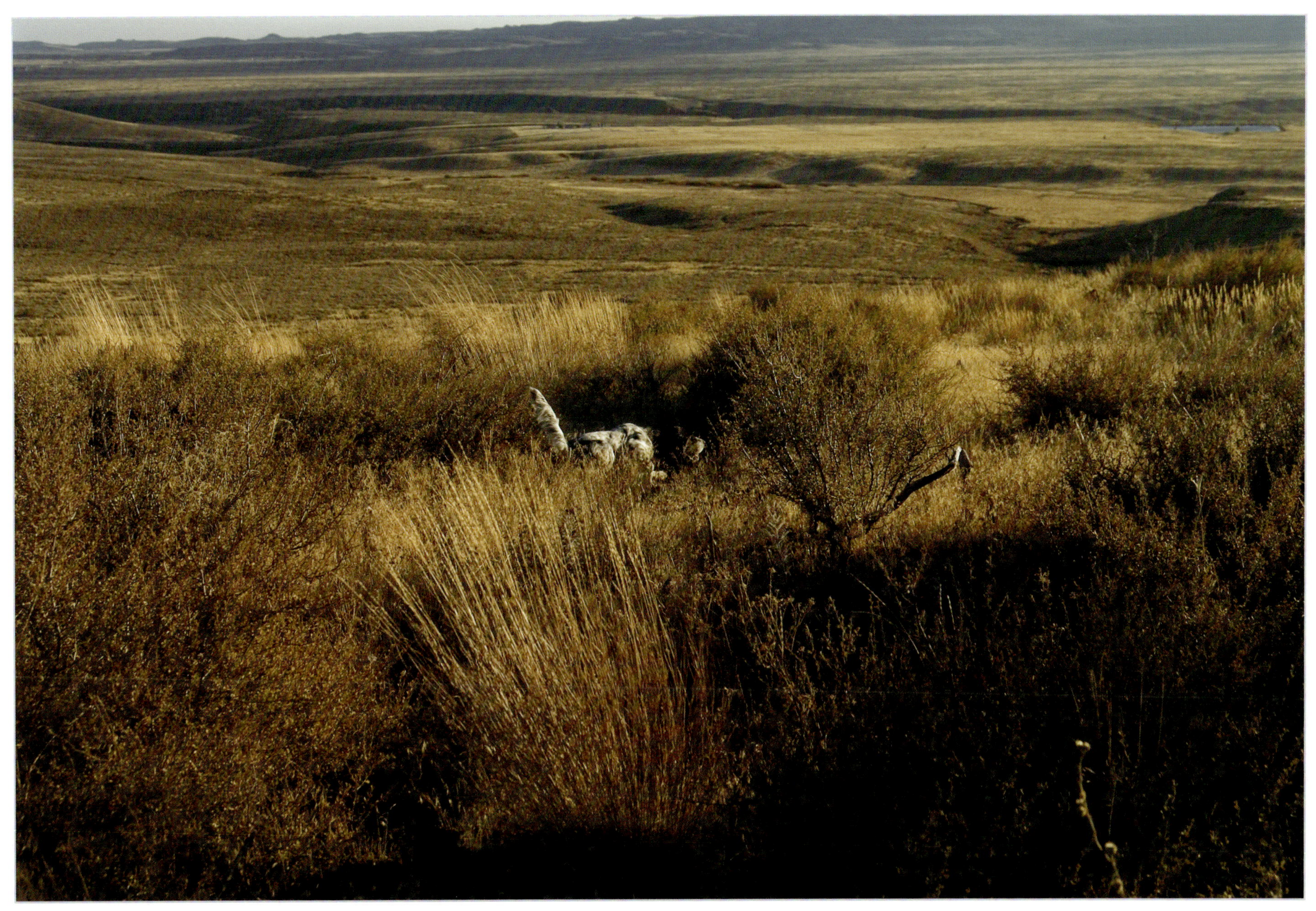

A photograph is a portrait painted by the sun. ~Unknown

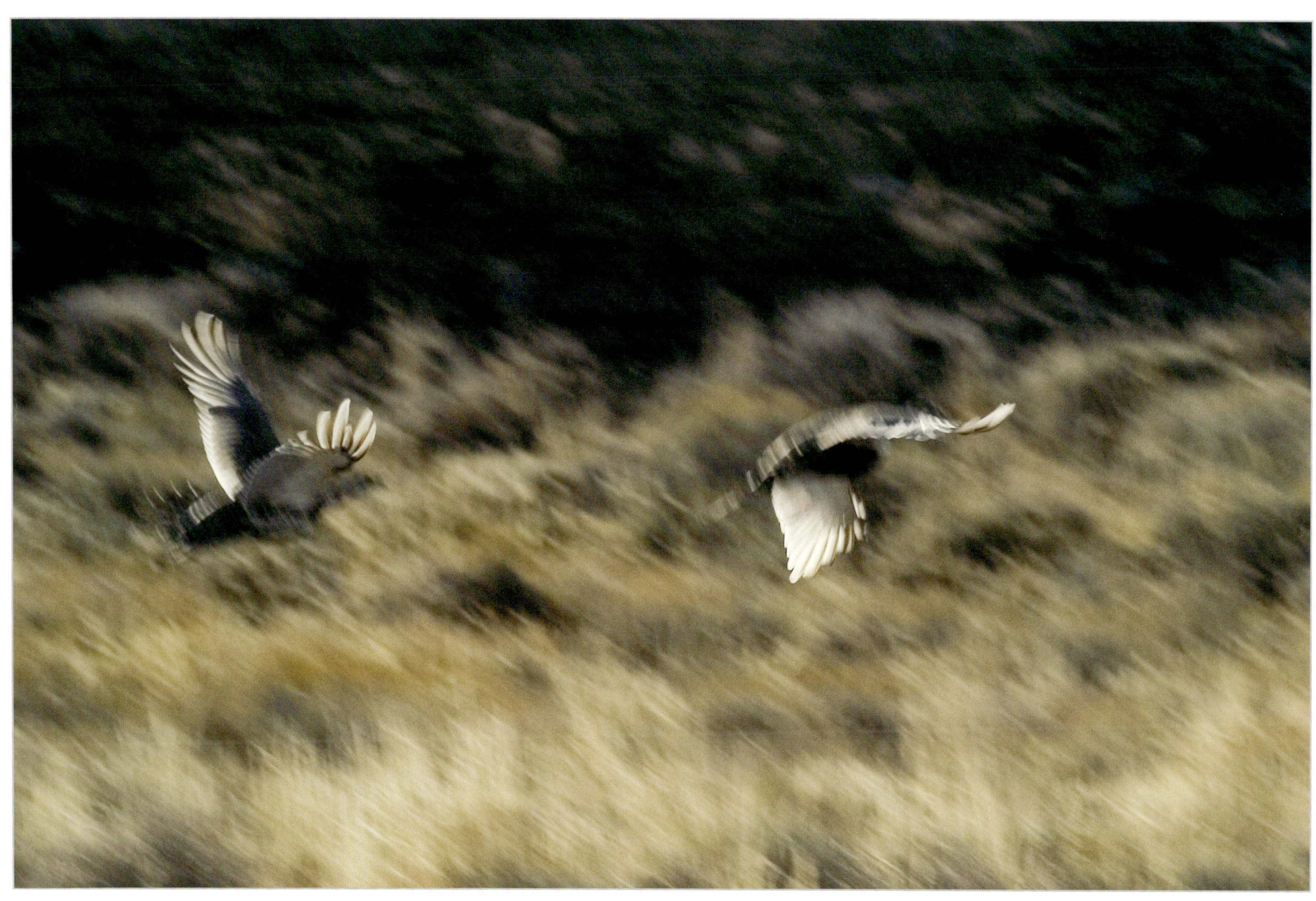

There are two ways to live; you can live as if nothing is a miracle; you can live as if everything is a miracle. ~Albert Einstein

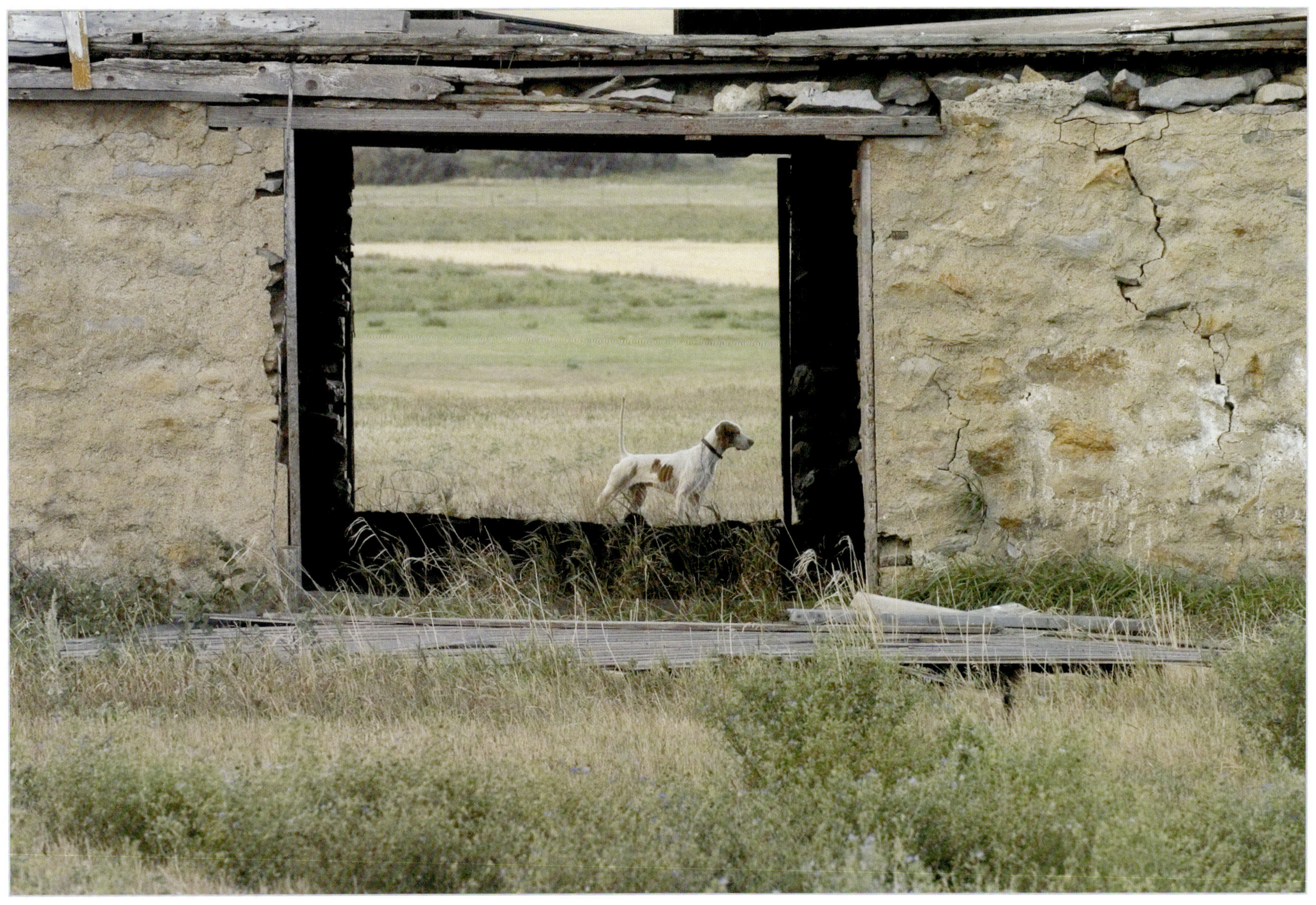

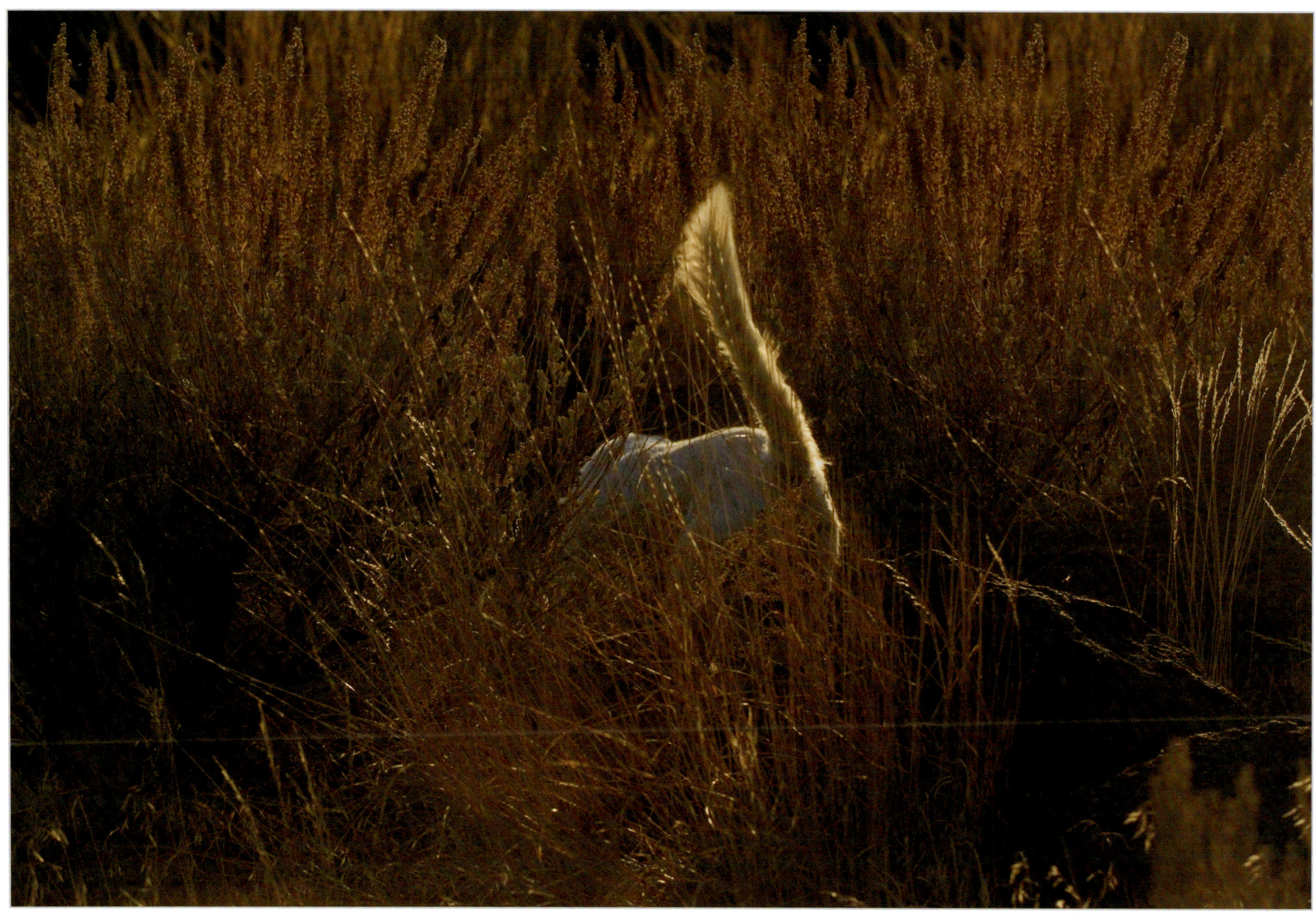

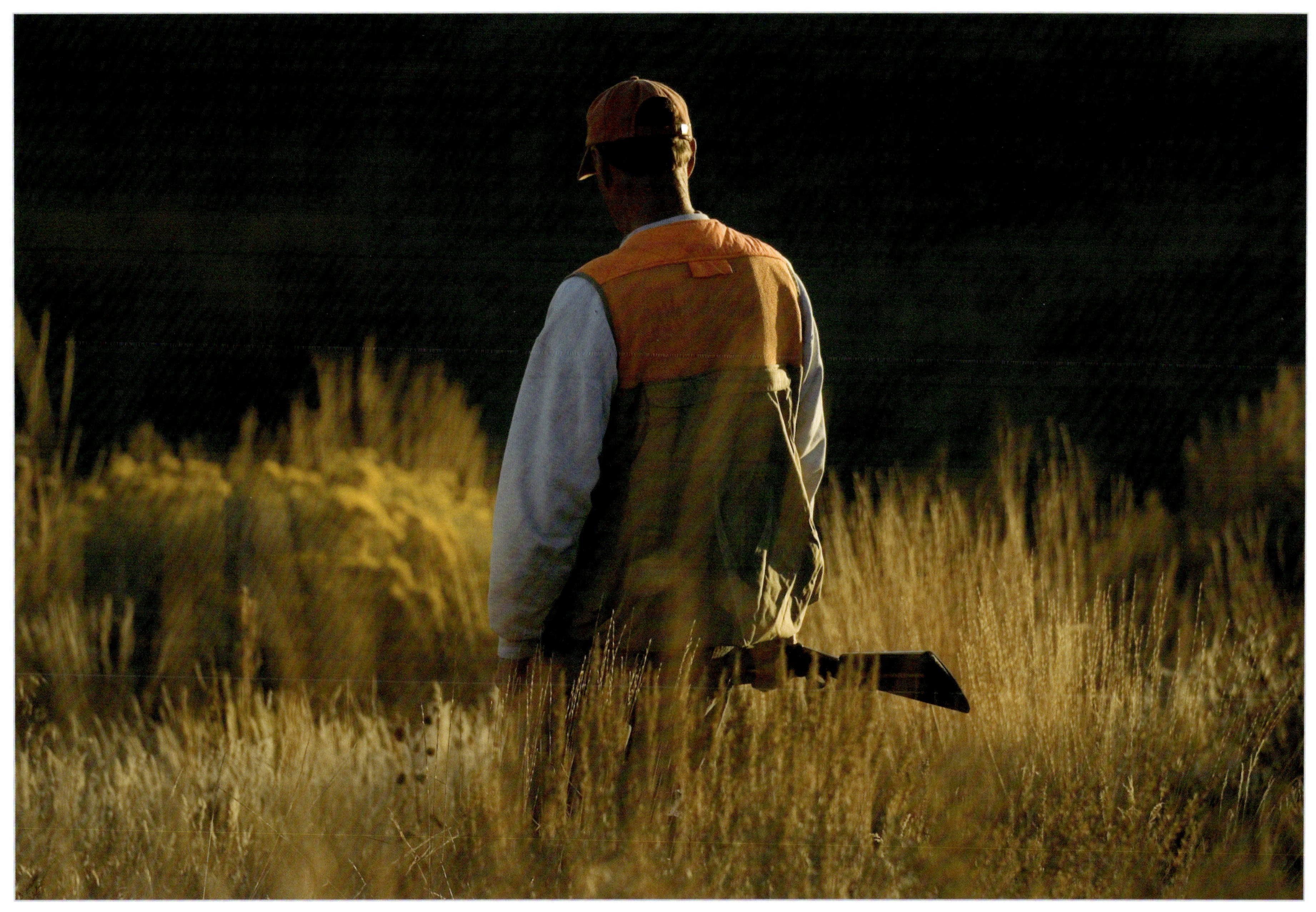

Moments of magic and mystery. ~C.E. Metz

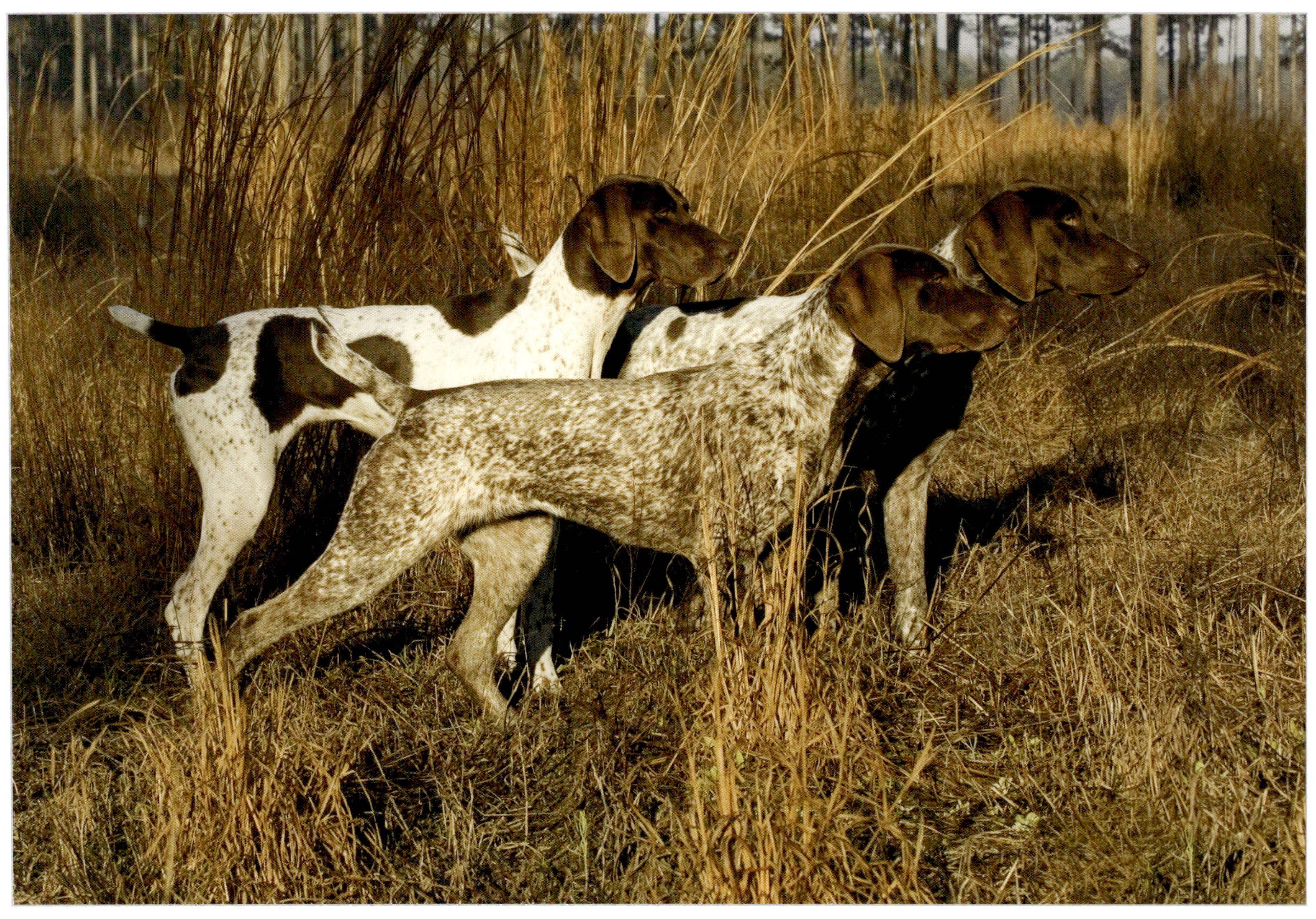

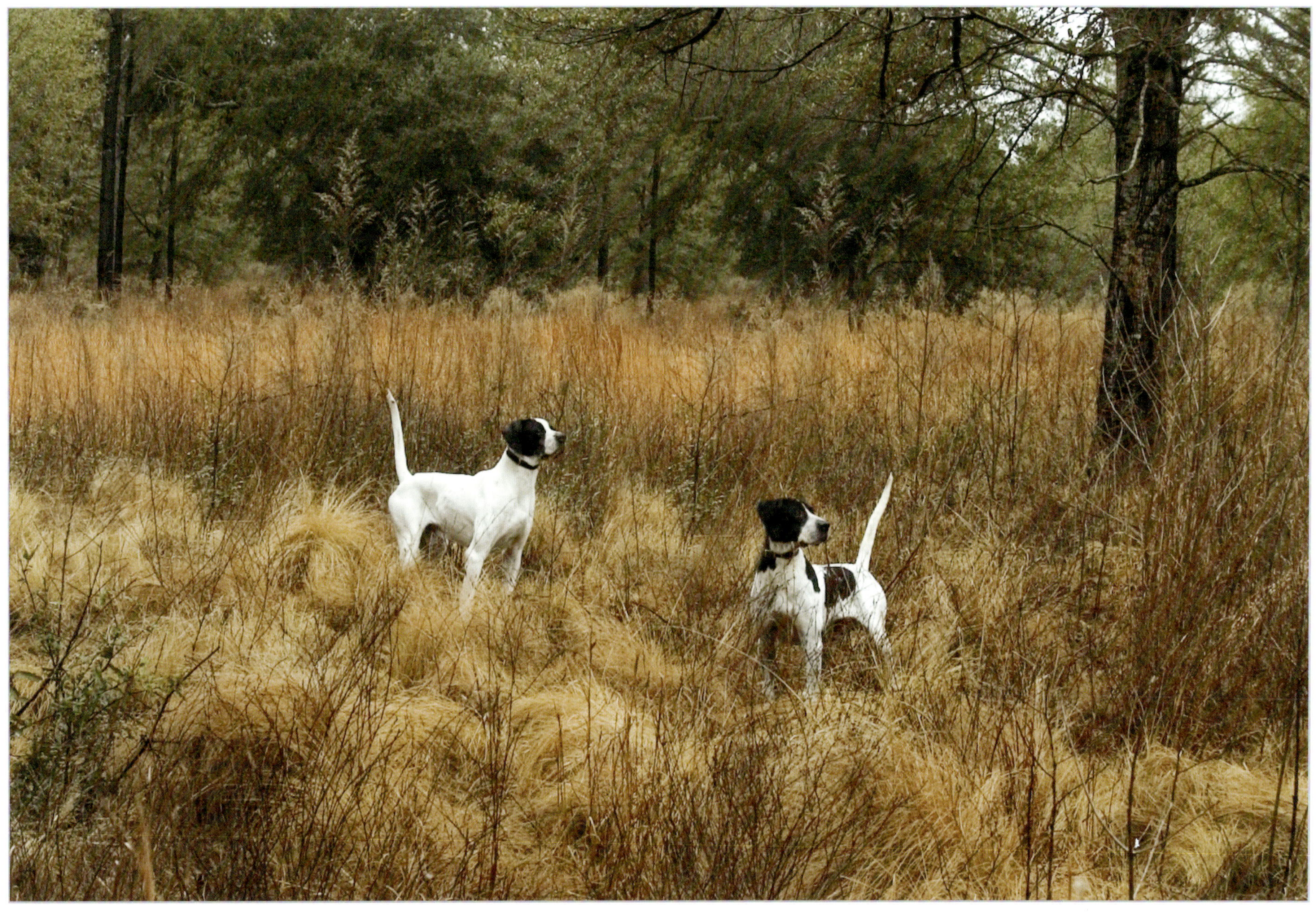

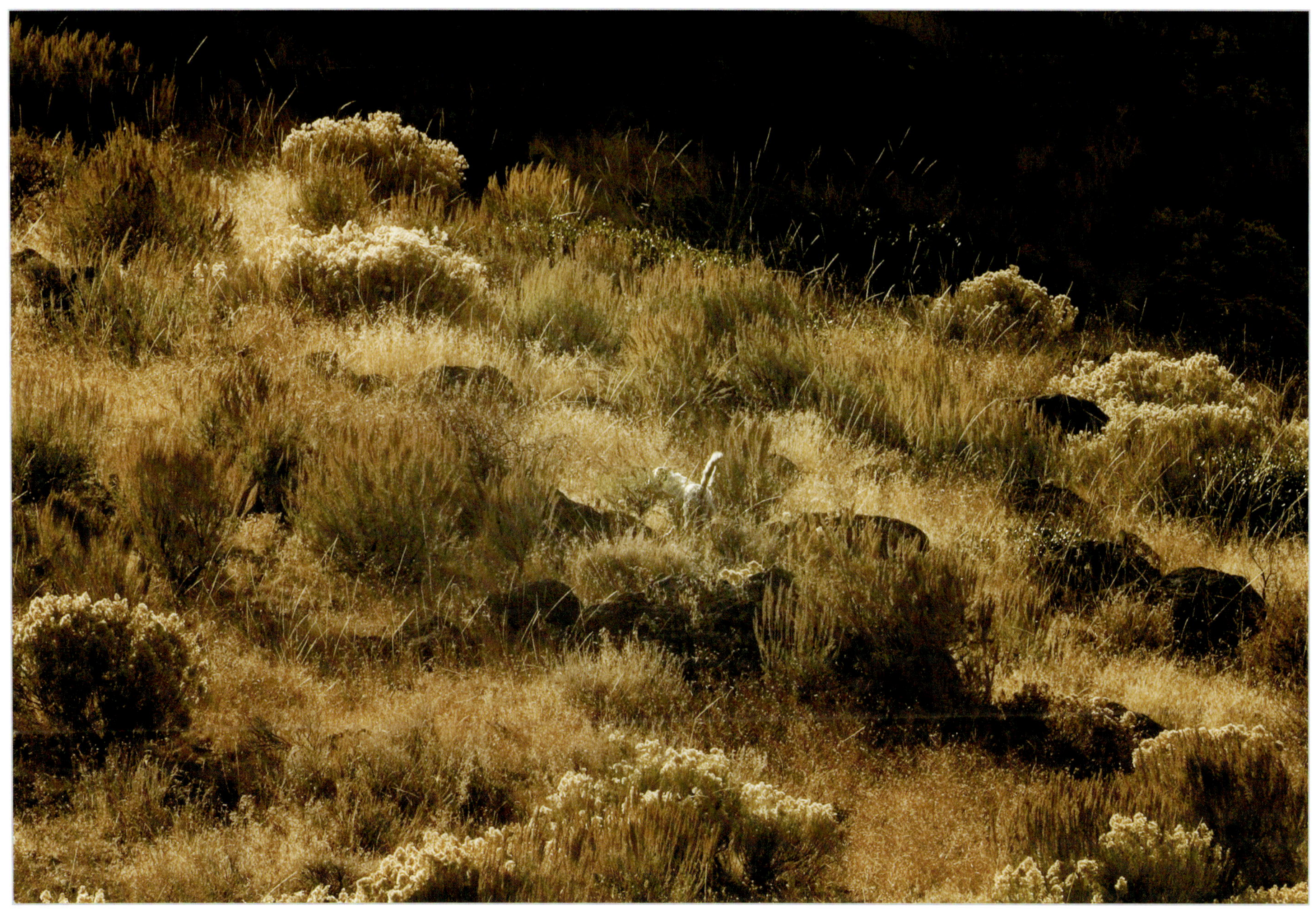

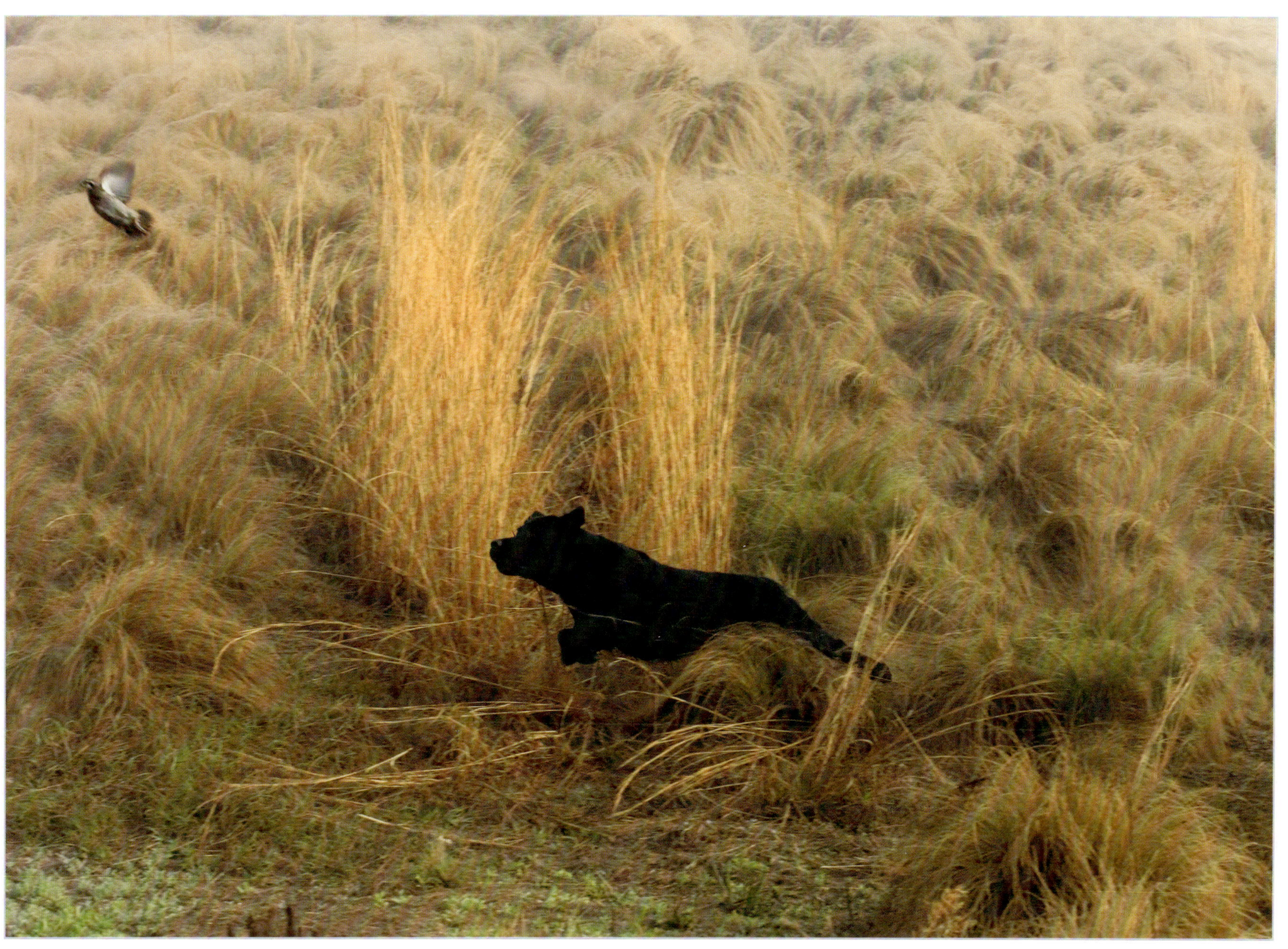

Dance is the landscape of a man's soul. ~Unknown

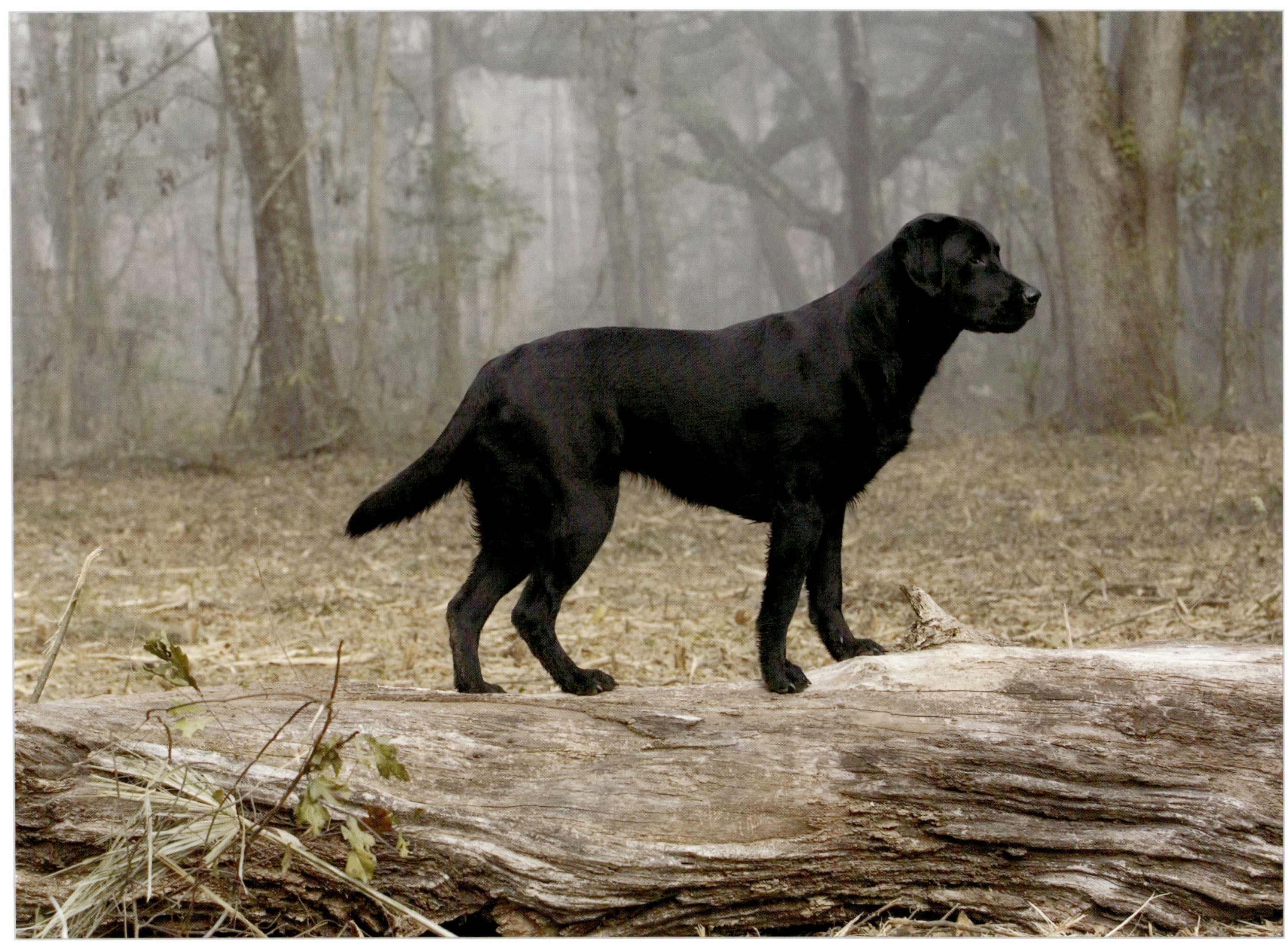

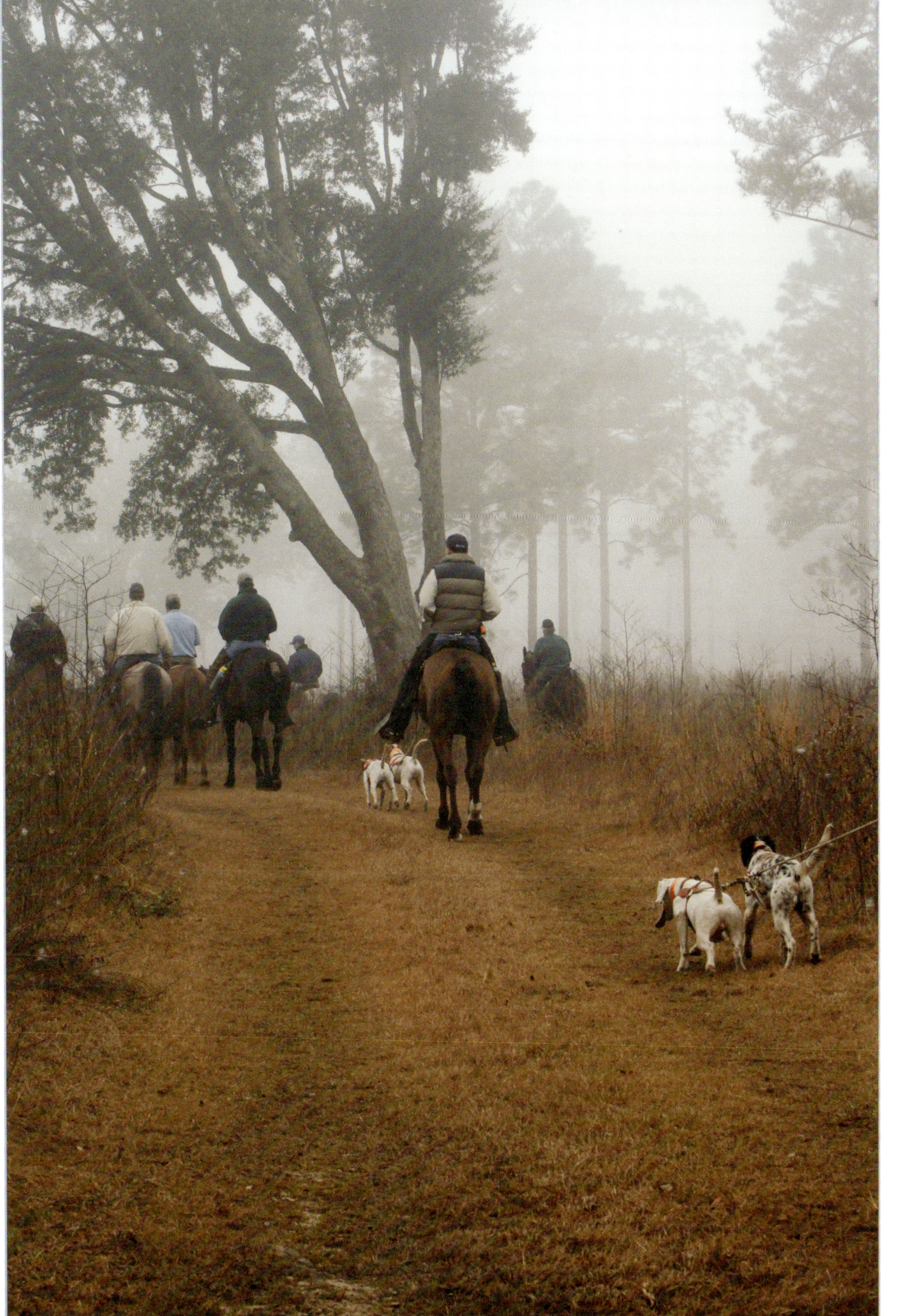

No matter how little money and how few possessions you own, having a dog makes you rich.
~Louis Sabin

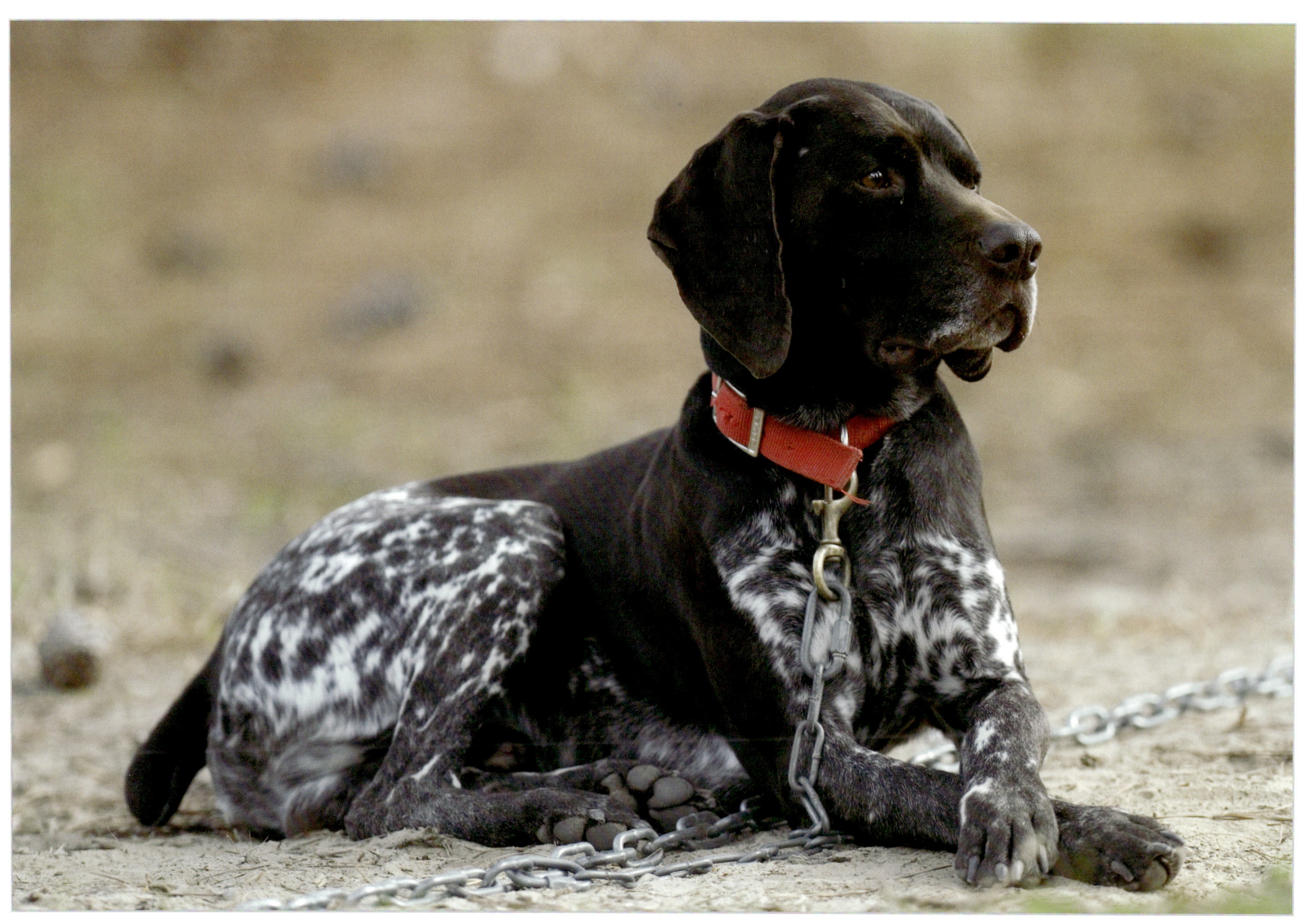

My goal in life is to become as wonderful as my dog thinks I am. ~Unknown

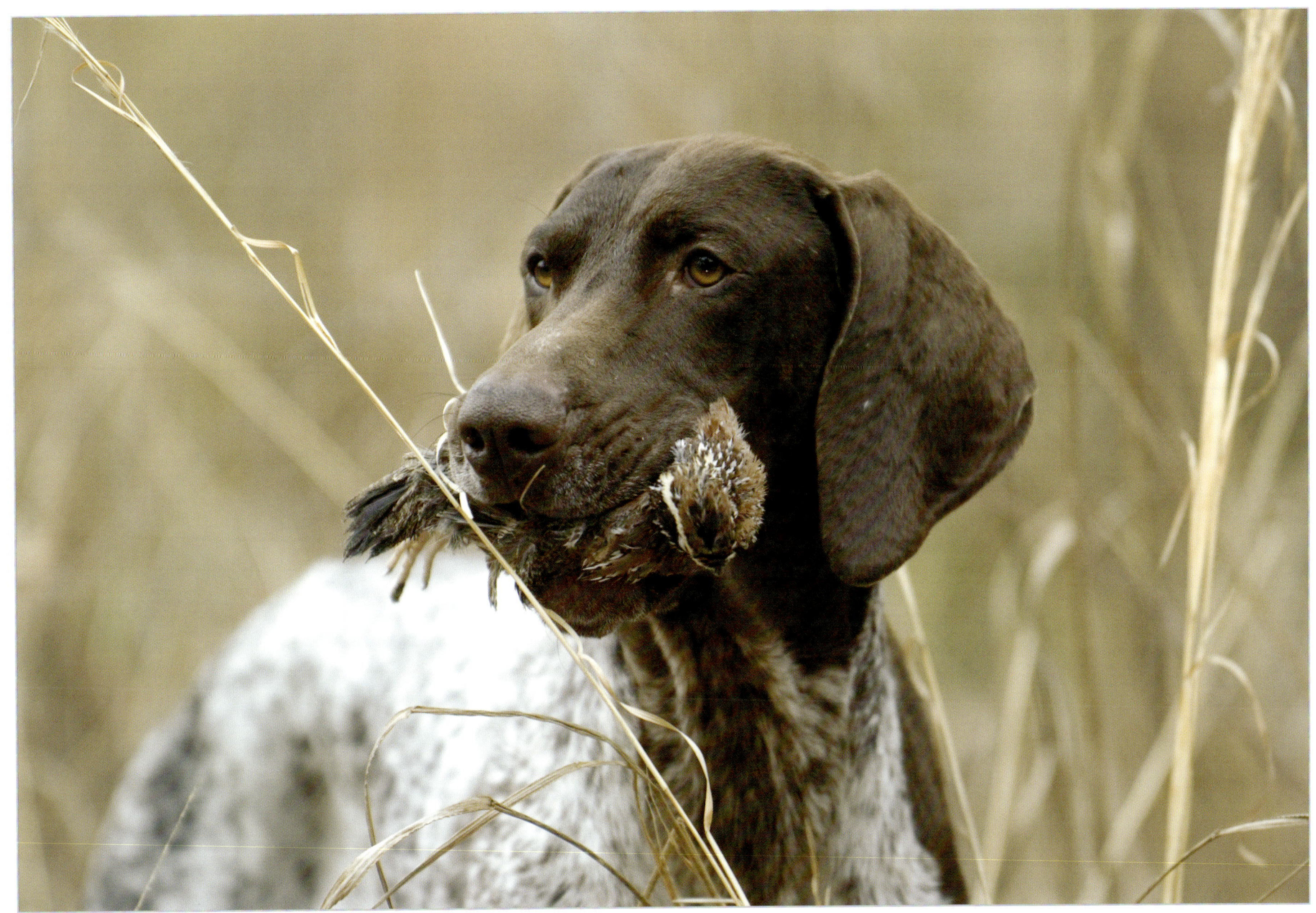

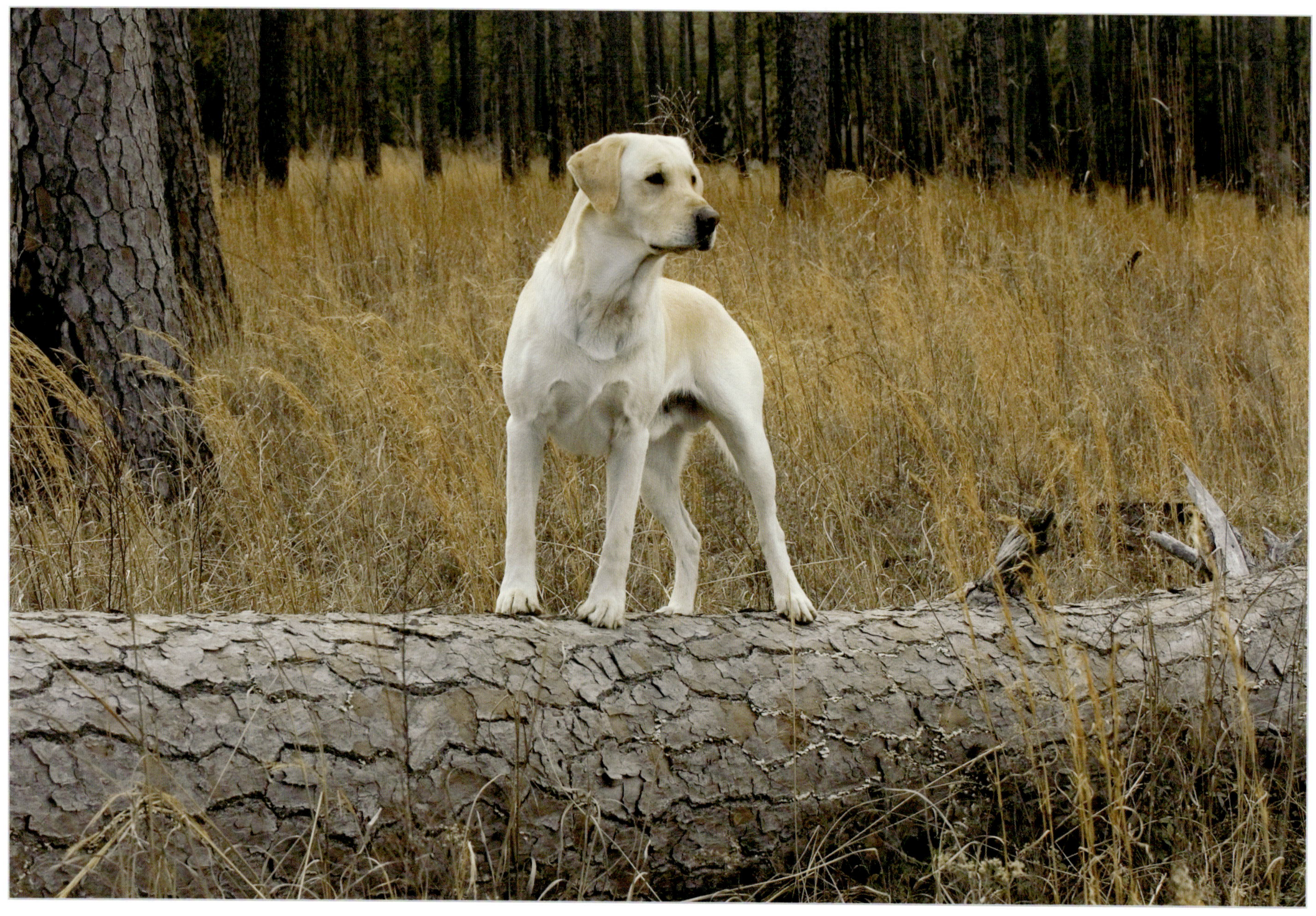

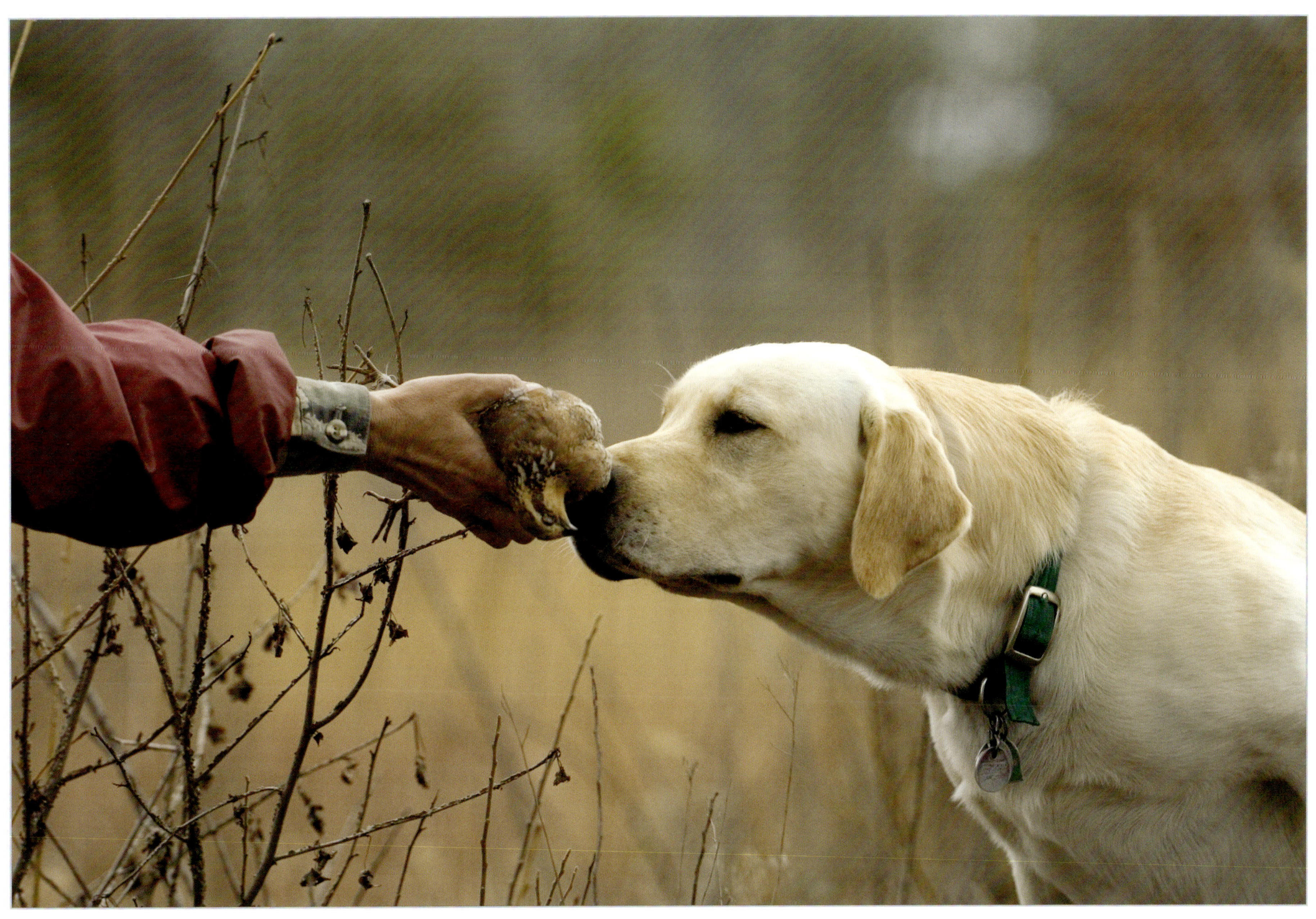

The mystery of scent. The moment of truth. ~C.E. Metz

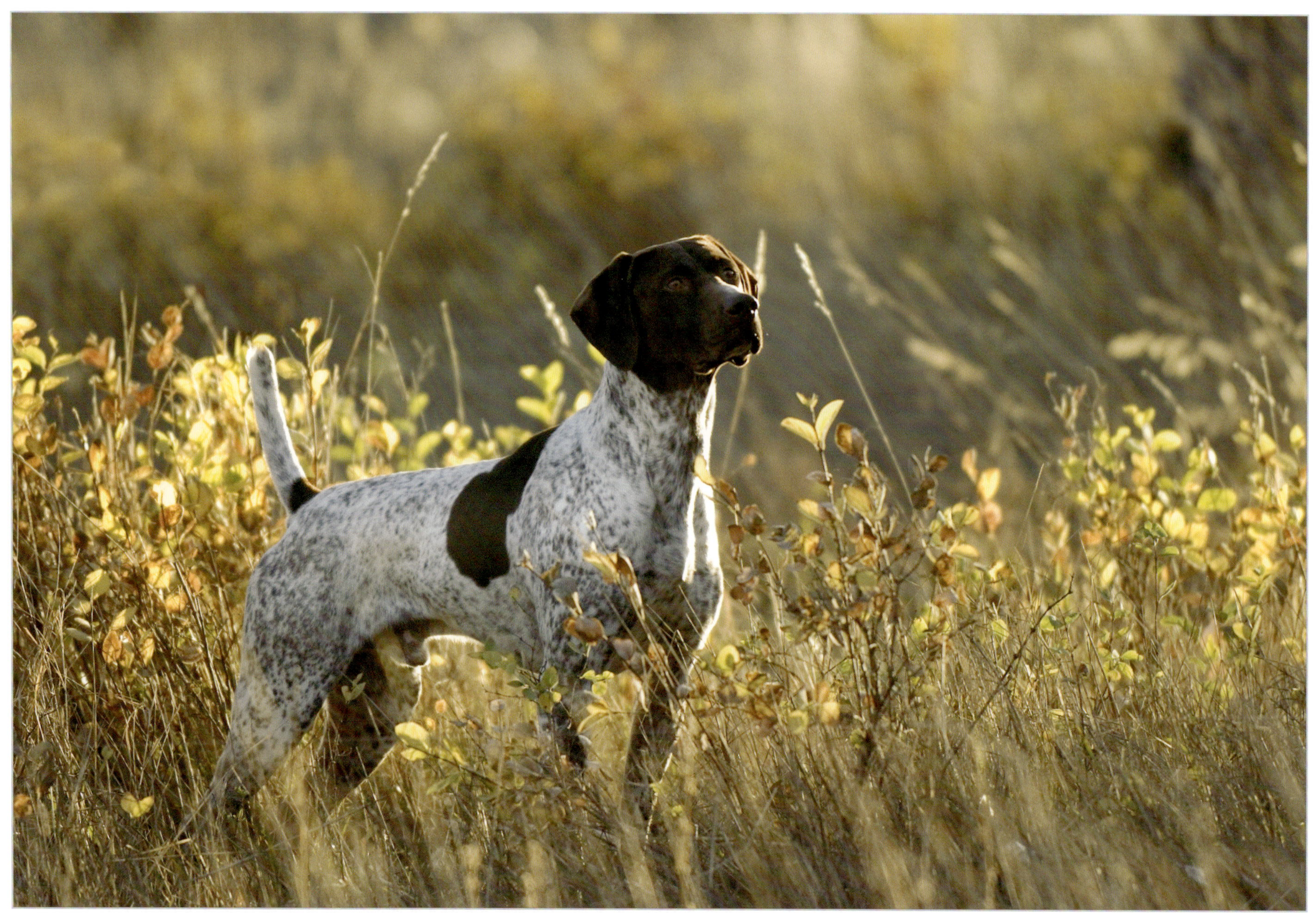

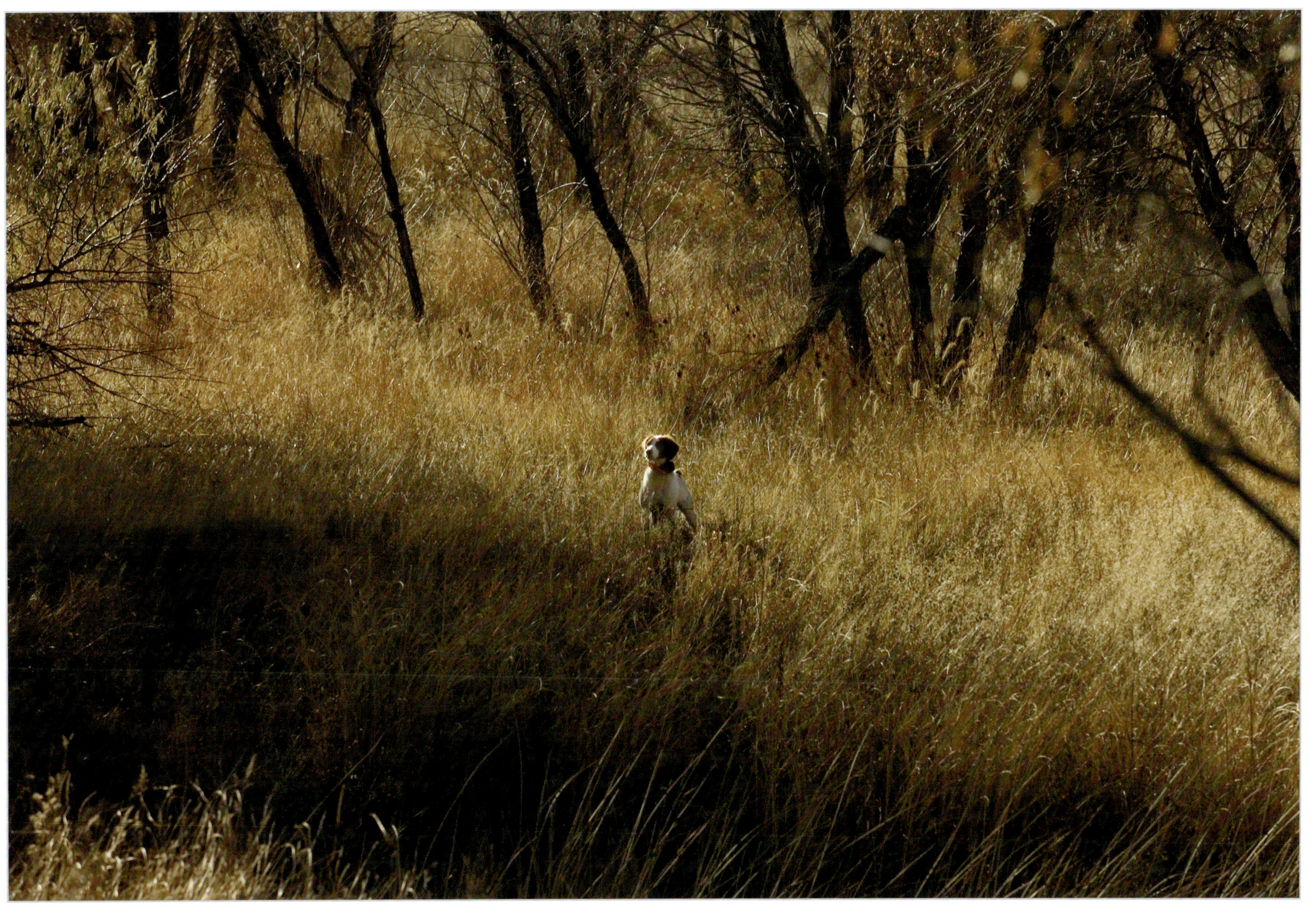

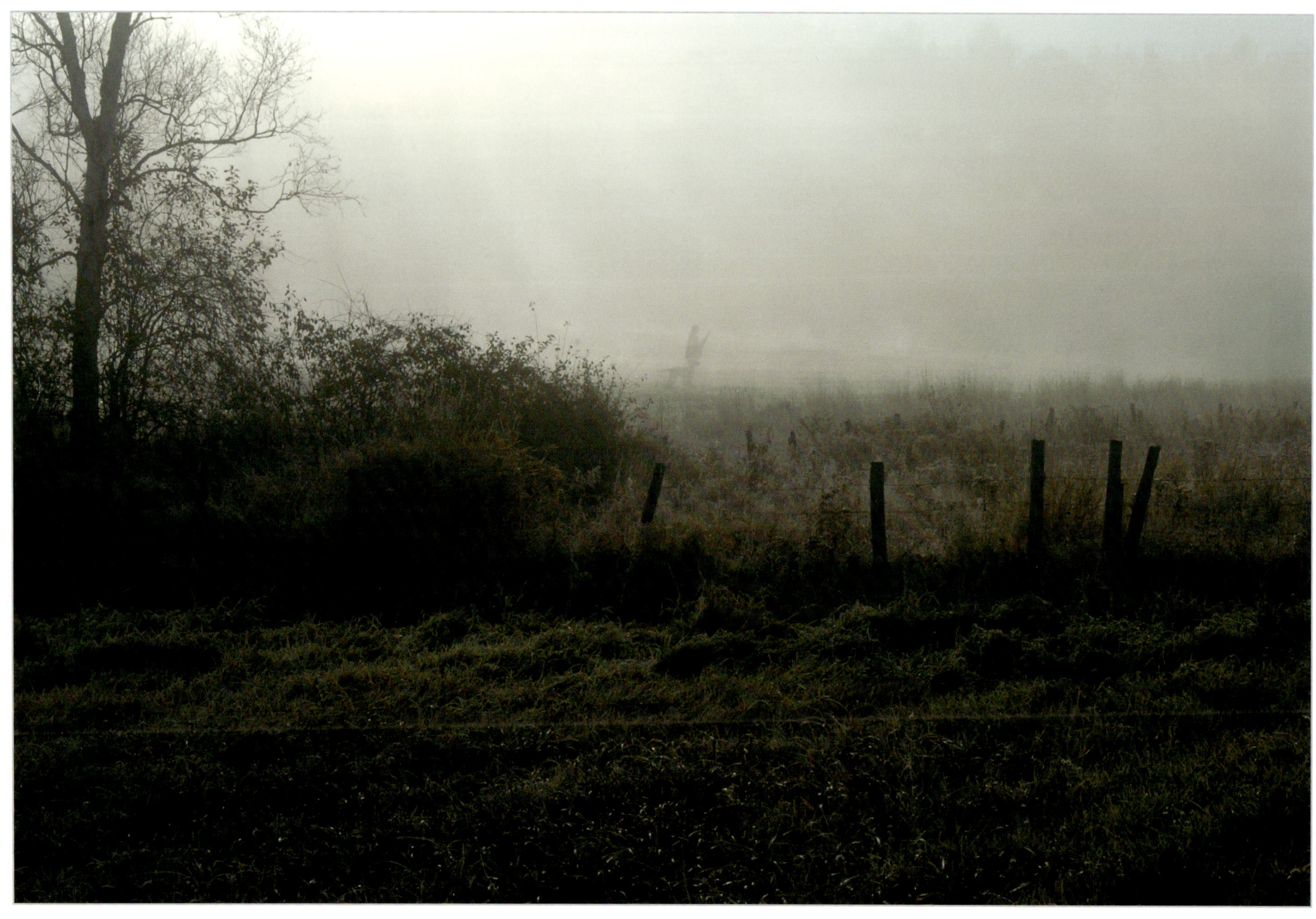

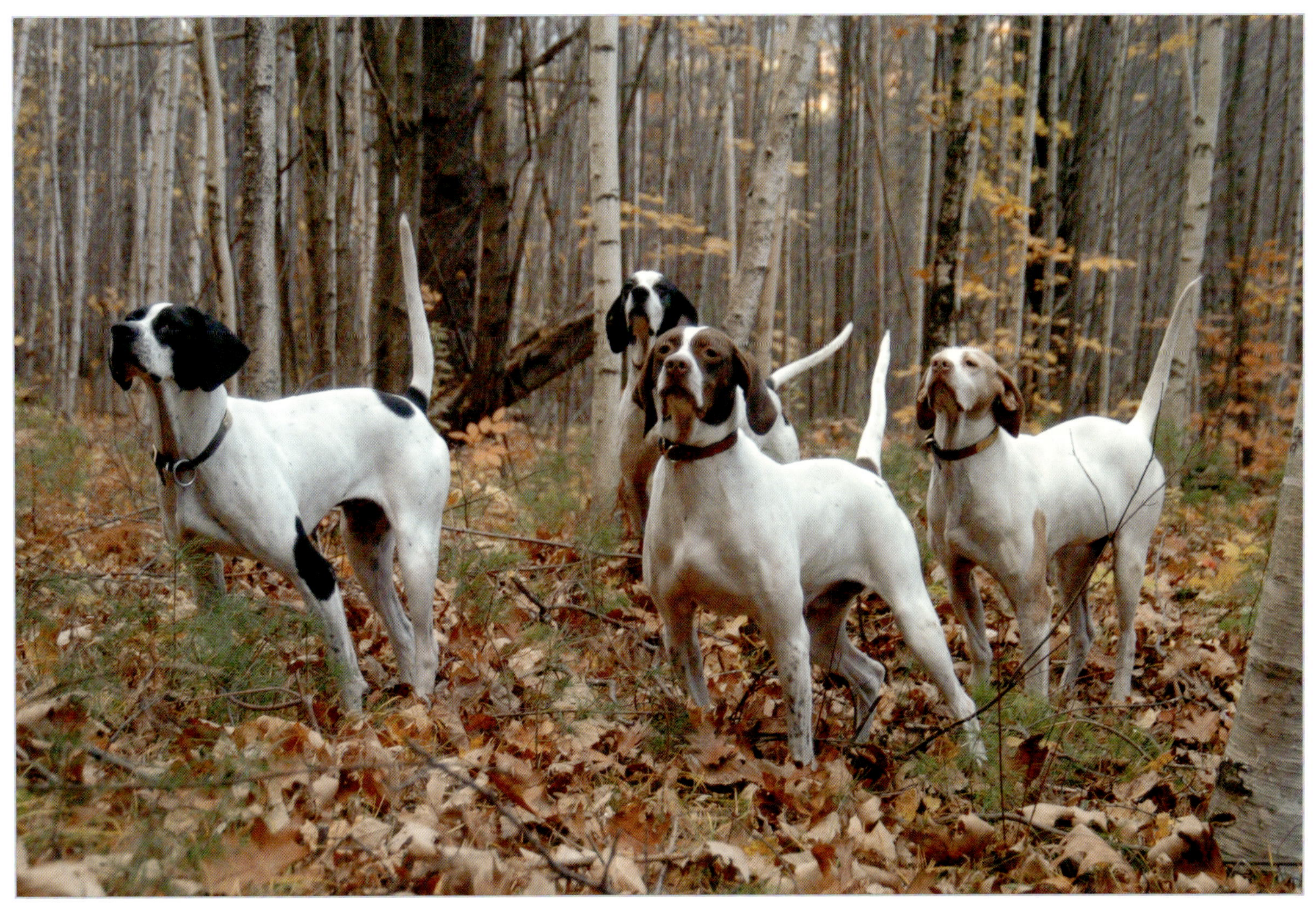

Do not follow where the path may lead. Go instead where there is no path, and leave a trail. ~Ralph Waldo Emerson

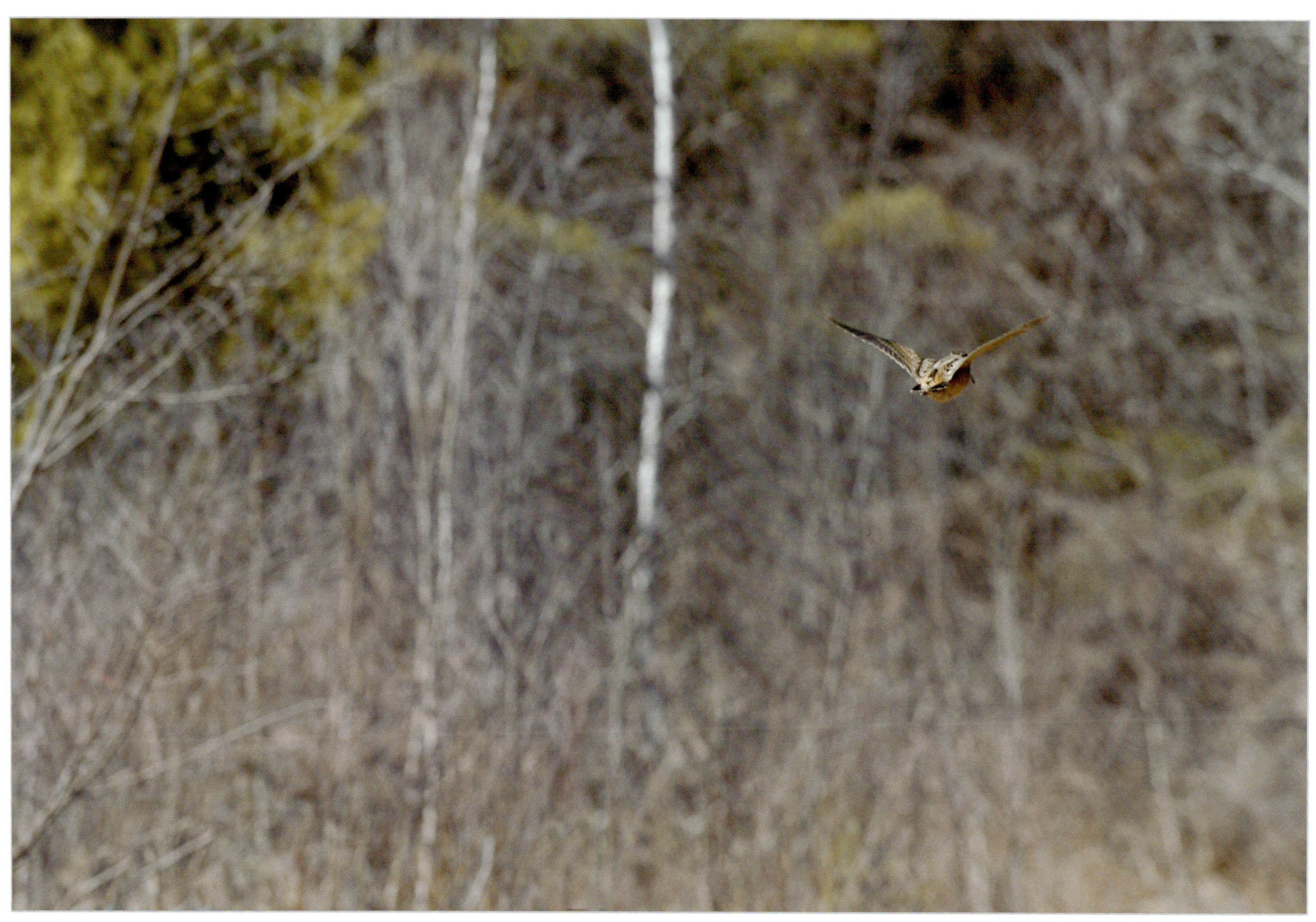

I have the simplest tastes. I am always satisfied with the best. ~Oscar Wilde

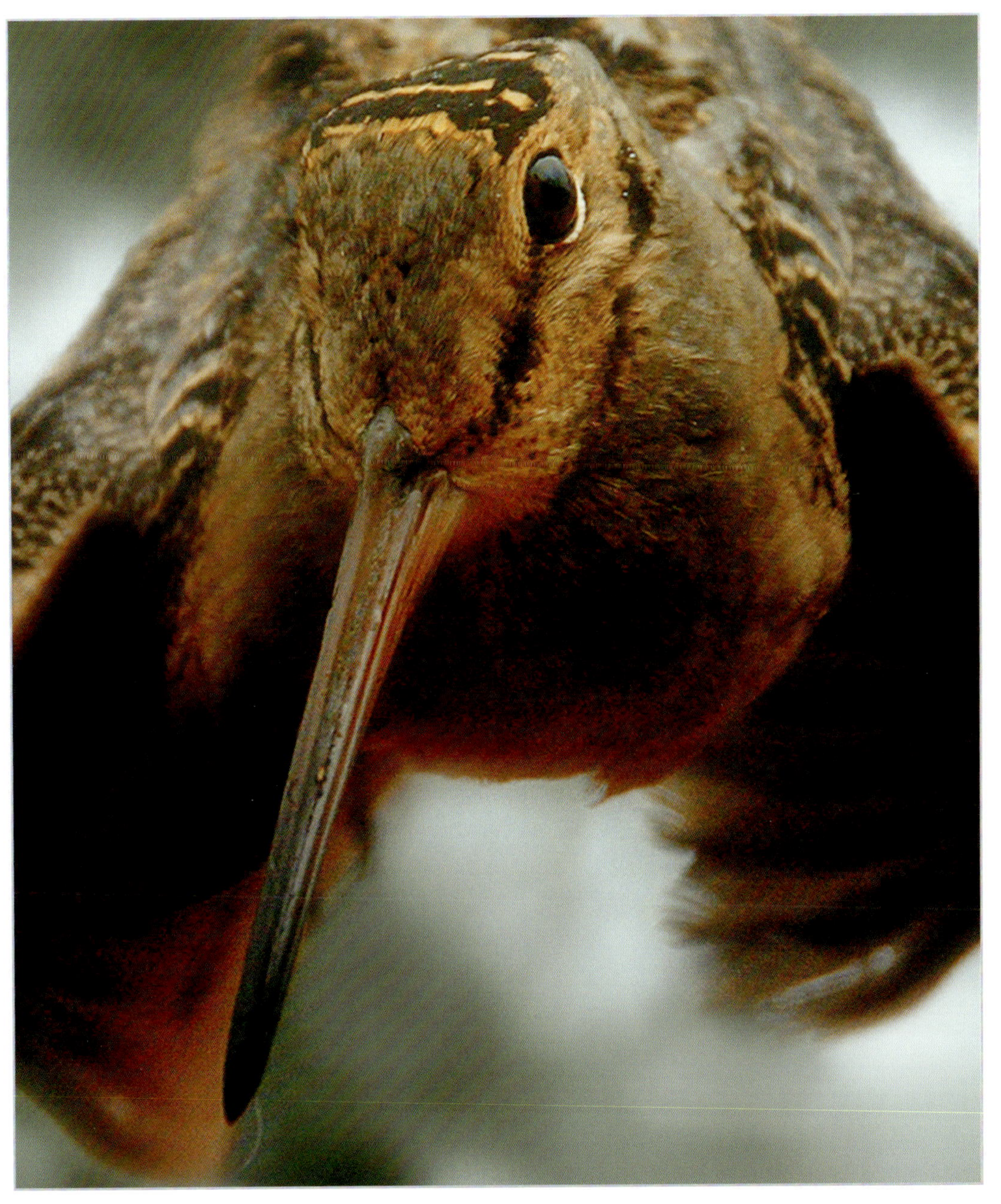

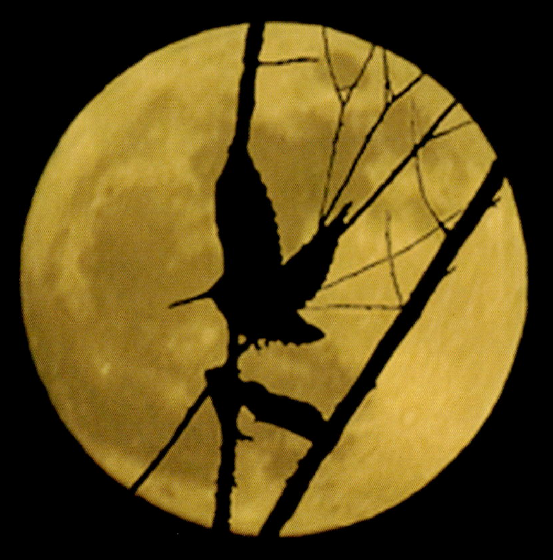

October is a symphony
of permanence and change.
~Bonaro W. Overstreet